Kundalini
and the
Art of Being

Kundalini
and the
Art of Being

Gabriel Morris

BARRYTOWN
STATION HILL

Published by Barrytown/Station Hill Press, Inc. in Barrytown, New York 12507, as a project of the Institute for Publishing Arts, Inc., in Barrytown, New York, a not-for-profit, tax-exempt organization [501(c)(3)], supported in part by grants from the New York State Council on the Arts.

E-mail: publishers@stationhill.org
Online catalogue: http://www.stationhill.org

Cover and interior design by Susan Quasha
Front cover photo by Roxanne Fischer
Back cover photo by Rana Ghahri-Saremi in Hampi, south India, February 2006

Chapter 1 of this book appeared as a book excerpt in *The Sedona Journal of Emergence* in November 2002.

Library of Congress Cataloging-in-Publication Data

Morris, Gabriel.
  Kundalini and the art of being / Gabriel Morris.
     p. cm.
  ISBN-13: 978-1-58177-096-4 (alk. paper)
  ISBN-10: 1-58177-096-0
  1. Morris, Gabriel. 2. Spiritual biography—United States. 3. Kundalini—Miscellanea. I. Title.
  BL73.M665A3 2007
  204'.36092—dc22
  [B]
                                        2007041339

Printed in the United States of America

To Mom, Dad and Christo;
and to Jeffrey,
and all my teachers

CONTENTS

INTRODUCTION

In the fall of 1994, I was twenty-two and leading a relatively stable life in rainy western Oregon, when I rather impulsively quit my job, sold my old Datsun pickup, moved out of my house, and hit the road with just my backpack on my back, thumb leading the way. I had only a vague notion of where I was going and what I was getting myself into. I simply had an undeniable yearning for adventure and the unknown, which I chose to follow. I was the type who tended to act on these sorts of impulses. Little did I know the real adventure that I was embarking on this time. Two months later—after hitchhiking partway across the country—I was staying with a friend in Texas with even less of an idea of what I was now doing in my vagabond existence than when I'd started my impulsive journey. It was nearing winter, I was almost broke, a long ways from home, and the living arrangement with my friend was less than ideal. And then, in the midst of meditation one evening, something subtle yet powerful shifted within my mind that changed my world forever. A sudden rush of energy flooded through me like nothing I'd ever before experienced or could have even imagined. I had no understanding then of what had occurred within my fragile consciousness. All I knew was that, in no more time than it takes for a bolt of lightning to strike, my experience and perception of reality had been utterly and irrevocably altered.

What happened to me in that pivotal moment actually had a name, although I didn't know it at the time—*Kundalini awakening*. I wish I could have known then that I wasn't just going crazy, but had experienced a spiritual breakthrough. At the time, however, I found myself cast abruptly into a psychological and physical hell, from which I found only temporary relief. I seemed to have, for no apparent reason, turned spontaneously schizophrenic. My spiritual quest of the past few years had inexplicably taken a painful and challenging turn, to say the least. The torment I experienced following my unanticipated Kundalini rising was so profound as to make me wonder if it was even worth enduring, just to live through another torturous day.

But fortunately, as surely as I'd fallen down a canyon of darkness within my soul, I managed to climb my way back out of it as well—to live to tell the tale, as they say. As those frightening first few days turned to weeks, and then months, I began to see a glimmer of light shine from within myself, that eventually proved to guide me back to something resembling sanity.

The following is the story of how I found myself in such a strange predicament—like many seekers these days stumbling rather blindly down the spiritual path—as well as how I managed to get myself out of it. Although I certainly didn't feel it initially, the awakening of the Kundalini energy is in actuality a great blessing. This I've discovered over the years, learning over time how to incorporate it into my daily life. Kundalini has the power to invigorate and evolve our spiritual beings like nothing else can, if we can just figure out how to handle it.

I'm not a qualified expert on this subject—just someone with a story to tell and a perspective to offer. My hope is that sharing my own experience will prove helpful to anyone struggling with this phenomenon, as well as to satisfy the curiosity of those interested in Kundalini, who may decide instead that they want nothing at all to do with its potent force, or perhaps be inspired to seek it out within themselves, and in so doing journey to the heart of the unknown.

PART 1

Electric Shock

CHAPTER 1

Late one December night, I lay meditating on my back at a friend's apartment in Austin, Texas, though I was far from being in a state of peace. Turbulent thoughts and feelings were rushing through me from the past days and weeks of emotional turmoil. I lay there in silent stillness, eyes closed, struggling to focus my scattered energy, searching for a place of serenity within myself so that I might drift gently into the solace of sleep and dreams.

Finding that place wasn't easy. There was such discordant energy coursing throughout my consciousness: chaotic, disturbing thoughts, deep feelings of fear and hopelessness, flashes of internal light, and random energy coming from somewhere within my mind. I lay unmoving despite my inner anguish, feeling it all, trying to let it flow through, willing myself to find that space of inner peace.

Finally, I touched something within myself that felt balanced and grounded beneath the confusion. It seemed real and connected, like a sturdy shelter amidst a powerful storm. I entered this place and pulled myself down beneath the turmoil.

I basked in relief as I ceased my struggling and allowed myself to relax into this tranquil place. I could feel the storm of my distress still raging all around me, but, for the time being, I was no longer engaged in resisting it. Its presence even seemed to diminish somewhat. I even indulged in this peace, wanting to hold onto it forever and not have to face the discomfort that I had managed to leave behind. Somehow I knew this could not be so.

I soon felt this quiet space begin to expand within and around me, engulfing me entirely. Then, abruptly, I began falling slowly downwards. At first, I was scared to be falling, but then, I realized that I enjoyed the feeling of drifting slowly down in quiet darkness and surrendered to it. The farther I fell, the more isolated my consciousness became. Soon I had completely forgotten about my previous turmoil. I only experienced myself falling down what seemed to be a narrow tunnel of darkness within my own mind.

Eventually I began to slow down. Finally I became still again amidst a vast darkness. I began moving around within this darkness to figure out where I was and stumbled across a memory. I was three years old, it was Halloween, and I was trick-or-treating with my father. We came to a dimly lit house with a long front walkway. My dad stood back near the street to let me walk up to the door on my own.

I walked timidly toward the door. It seemed like such a long way and I was a little scared, especially with the dull front porch light. Finally I got to the door, reached up, and rang the doorbell.

It chimed pleasantly, reassuring me. The door opened, and a woman was standing there, reaching into a big brown paper bag of assorted candy on a small table by the door.

"Trick-or-treat!" I said, proud of myself for having met the challenge, raising up my own quarter-full bag of candy.

"Why, aren't you a cute little boy," she said. "Well, here you go…" She dropped a few pieces of candy into my bag.

"Don't forget to say thank you," my dad called out from the street.

"Thank you," I said.

"You're quite welcome," she said as she smiled and slowly closed the door.

I turned to step down from the front porch. Just then, a shadow loomed over me as a man leapt out from the darkness of a nearby bush—arms raised overhead, mouth and eyes wide open, and gave a blood-curdling scream, like a banshee about to pounce on his victim.

I screamed, terrified, dropped my bag of candy and ran crying to my father.

"Hey, kid, c'mon—I was just joking around," the man said, suddenly feeling apologetic.

My dad was furious. He marched up to him from the sidewalk, shaking a fist. "What the hell is your problem, you asshole, scaring little kids like that?" He seemed on the verge of punching the guy in the face, having been almost as surprised and scared by the event as myself.

"I'm sorry," said the man, cowering a little, clearly regretting his actions now. "It was just a Halloween prank."

"Yeah, real funny, scaring little kids half to death..." He reached down to grab my bag of candy from the front steps and walked away muttering, "Stupid goddamn jerk...some people..." as he took my hand. We walked back home through the night as I cried, still baffled by what had just occurred.

As I lay on the apartment floor deep in meditation, I relived this scene as if I were actually there. I felt the intense fear that had engulfed me and remembered that it had stayed with me for a long time. For weeks afterward I had talked about the boogeyman at night, afraid of going to sleep with the lights out.

I became so involved with reliving this childhood memory, that I completely forgot about my present situation. I was brought back to my body by a sudden, subtle movement at the base of my spine. My mind went instinctively to this movement to see what it was. As I brought my attention there, I felt the ball of energy move again. Then I felt it rise slightly, as if it were trying to move up my spine.

I had a sense that this energy moving at the base of my spine—whatever it was—was somehow connected to the intense feelings of fear I was reliving in my childhood memory. I thought that perhaps if I allowed this ball of energy to flow completely through me, the process would dissolve all the unpleasantness associated with the memory and I would be left with a feeling of contentment in its place.

I concentrated on this energy at the base of my spine until I felt it move again. It felt something like a bubble moving up a straw. It rose slowly but steadily, as if it were being sucked up by something. It paused for a moment as it came to my neck and the base of my skull and then exploded into my brain.

At that moment, I was assaulted by a rush of energy so powerful that I literally thought it might kill me. It seemed to last an eternity and yet only for an instant. It felt much like an explosion or an electric shock. I surrendered to this sudden flood of energy as it engulfed me, because it was so unanticipated that I had no time to even attempt to resist it.

As the rushing sensation eventually began to subside, I was relieved to find that I had survived. I hoped that the gentle, peaceful presence I had anticipated would now replace the terrible and unexpected shock I had just received, but unfortunately, I couldn't have been more wrong. I was horrified to find an overwhelming terror roaring into my consciousness that, for the moment, eradicated from my memory my earlier recollection of childhood fear. An ever-mounting, cascading, crashing wave of crushing terror overtook me, as if a dam had broken between my conscious and subconscious minds and I were being flooded by unresolved experiences and feelings buried deep within my soul. I waited for these overwhelming feelings either to render me unconscious or else to pass through me and then subside. But they did neither.

As the minutes wore on, the erratic energies crashing through me became only more intense and unbearable. I was soon consumed by the wish that I hadn't done whatever it was I had just done. My previous emotional turmoil—and even the frightening childhood memory— were but feathers compared to the incredible weight of psychosis that was now beginning to descend on me.

I soon began to notice within myself more explosions of energy, like aftershocks of an earthquake. They came as if from the darkness of my own mind, closer and closer to my conscious awareness until I was hit by a steady wave of electric shocks in successively increasing intensity.

As I lay there on my back feeling crushed, bombarded, and overpowered by something I couldn't even identify or locate in my consciousness, I kept thinking, "This has to subside, this has to go away eventually, this can't go on much longer." Yet, even as I was telling myself this, the force of energy was increasing. Whatever this disturbing power was that I had somehow brought into my consciousness, it seemed it wasn't going away any time soon. The brief moment of peace and comfort I'd experienced during my meditation felt now like a fading mirage of some kind—a calm before the storm, a temporary stillness before the harsh and chaotic reality set in.

Finally, I got up from the floor, where I'd also been sleeping the past few weeks, and began pacing back and forth, wracking my brain to make sense of what had just happened. My rational mind tried to come up with a plausible explanation for my sudden predicament. I went over what I had just experienced—a ball of energy moving up my spine while meditating that then flowed into my brain. I came to the conclusion that there must be some sort of bodily fluid residing in the spine, that wasn't supposed to be anywhere near the brain. Somehow I must have released this fluid, causing it to flow into my brain, creating a chemical reaction of sorts. Although this flimsy explanation managed to calm me momentarily, it did nothing to alter my painful psychological symptoms.

Since it seemed that I wasn't going to be falling asleep all that quickly, I put on some warm clothes and left the apartment to go for a walk and get some fresh air. I hoped at least to distract myself from whatever it was that had just occurred. It brought me some relief just to get out of the cramped apartment, but when I came back to the apartment and sat down at the dining room table, I realized that my symptoms had not diminished. My physical activity seemed to have increased the flow of energy coming from the base of my spine, further intensifying the painful sensations within both my body and mind. Sitting down and trying to relax increased my discomfort as well, as my mind instinctively focused on the source of the pain, desiring to alleviate it but, instead, giving it more power by its attention.

I had a fiery sensation at the base of my spine. I felt that I had to stay continually focused on holding down this fire. I was afraid that letting it rise freely would mean receiving more overpowering energy. My heart was pounding and skipping beats. I was now receiving electric shocks at the tops of my feet and the backs of my hands as well as from unknown places within my consciousness. I felt as if some force was pulling away at my temples, trying to extract my life essence; and I had a crushing sensation around my head, as if my skull was in the grip of a large wrench. The fire at the base of my spine was spreading upwards despite my attempts to control it, engulfing my entire back in raging heat and pain. And the electric shocks coming from my hands and feet were spreading through my limbs to my torso, so that it felt as if the nerves, bones, and muscles in my body were becoming electrically charged.

I decided to lie down on my thin mattress on the floor and try to fall asleep. I hoped at least that unconsciousness would provide me with some temporary relief, but I found that, although exhausted from a day that had been emotionally draining to begin with only to escalate into a state of severe psychic imbalance, I was still unable to sleep. Instead, I lay there through the night enduring my inner torment, tossing and turning, praying to drift into unconsciousness to ease my pain, or at least for the strength to regain my sanity in the following days.

If I had known at the time that it would not be days or weeks, but years before I found myself in a state of mind that I could call manageable, I doubt if I could have survived the awesome journey on which I had just embarked. I had no understanding then of what had just occurred or what might have caused it. I didn't know that this was a legitimate and well-documented spiritual phenomenon. Though I had practiced yoga and was familiar with the term *Kundalini*, I didn't realize that this intense onslaught of energy originating in the base of the spine was what it actually referred to. I didn't know that there was a positive side to this experience, bringing spiritual healing and well-being. All I knew was that, for no reason that I could fathom, my fundamental experience of reality had just been shattered—as if I'd been struck by lightning out of a clear blue sky, and I was reeling in shock from its damaging effects on my body, mind, and soul, struggling to stay alive.

As the light of dawn finally began to emerge the next day, I awoke from restless sleep to find that my symptoms had not subsided. I decided to get out of the small apartment for the day despite my exhaustion, hoping to distract myself.

The reasons why I found myself in Austin, Texas were rather complex. But to make a long story short (for now), Amy—the friend whose apartment I was sharing—was actually an ex-girlfriend of sorts, with whom I was not in the best of communication at the time. She was seeing someone else, while I was staying with her temporarily in her one-room studio. But she was the only person in the state whom I could call a friend. The emotional turmoil that opened this story was a result of this predicament, making my life situation at the time a rather dismal one, even before this bizarre development. But I'll elaborate more on that later.

I spent most of that day wandering around Austin, in a dazed and hyper-conscious state. By that afternoon, my exhaustion had intensified my symptoms so much that I was unsure if I could stand it much longer. In addition to the terrifying psychological imbalance, the blocked energy was also manifesting more and more as pain in my body. My heart alternately wrenched, stopped, stuttered, and pulsated wildly, so that I was wandering along downtown Austin with my hand clutching my chest as if that might somehow keep it from stopping altogether. The burning at the base of my spine was constant, and I was receiving electric shocks at random throughout my body.

Eventually, later that afternoon, I decided to head back to Amy's apartment. I was relieved to find that she wasn't there, since I wouldn't have known what to say or how to relate to her in my present condition. I took a shower, then lay down on my mattress on the floor to take a nap. Finally, miraculously, I was able to fall into a deep sleep.

When I awoke later that evening, I actually felt a little better, momentarily. But everything flooded back as I fully awoke. I also experienced a moment of panic as I remembered that I had a job at a nearby deli and I might be late for work. The moment of relief I felt after calling in—to find that I wasn't working until the next evening—was little comfort, as it left me with the dilemma of what to do with myself through that evening and the next day.

I went for a long walk in the evening air. I came back later that night to find Amy there, already asleep with the lights out. I crawled into my sleeping bag on the floor and closed my eyes. Once again, I tossed and turned for hours, unable to relax. Finally, I fell into a few hours of fitful sleep.

I awoke to the morning light dawning through the curtains. As before, my tormenting symptoms descended on me rapidly as I came back to waking consciousness. I also felt a deep exhaustion, with hardly enough energy to get out of my sleeping bag. I gathered the strength to get up from my spot on the floor, put on some clothes, and eat half a bowl of cereal. I was unable to finish it, however, because the simple act of eating seemed to be the cause of disturbing electrical sensations throughout my mouth and throat that scared the appetite right out of me. I left the apartment and spent another day wandering aimlessly around Austin, praying constantly for relief from my situation, or at least for some understanding of what I could do to alleviate my distress.

That evening, I had to work my shift at the deli. Given my predicament, I wasn't sure how I would tolerate spending eight hours making sandwiches and cordially ringing up orders for customers. I decided at least to show up and give it a try—perhaps it would help bring me back to normalcy. If it didn't, I would come up with an excuse to leave.

The physical surroundings at work that evening—the bright lights and plastic surroundings—greatly magnified my already distorted perceptions. After a few hours of somehow performing my duties, I started feeling totally overwhelmed due to both the unnatural environment of the restaurant and the necessity to hide everything that I was experiencing internally. I was literally beginning to feel as if my body were about to lose its ability to function. I was a 30-watt light bulb being hit by 90 watts of electricity—and it felt as if I were shorting out.

The pressure on my skull was so intense that I thought it might actually be damaging my brain. My bones felt like electrified metal, and I had the sensation of a steel spike penetrating my body at the top of my head, driven all the way down through my crotch and sticking out between my legs. My very consciousness seemed to be trying to separate from my body, as if I were about to fly uncontrollably onto the astral planes.

Finally, I told the one other employee I was working alongside that I had to leave because I was feeling sick. I abruptly left the restaurant and began walking in the direction of Amy's apartment. As I passed by a public phone, I decided to call 911. I had no doubt right then that my situation was an emergency—if I could just manage to explain what it was.

I dialed and asked to speak to a medical professional. When I got one on the line, I tried to relate my predicament to her. I proposed the spinal-fluid theory that I had come up with earlier, hoping it might be a genuine medical problem she could help me with. Although she tried her best to understand my condition, her basic response was, "I'm sorry, but I don't quite understand what your problem is…"

I hung up and decided to call my dad. It was comforting to hear his voice at the other end of the line though, understandably, he couldn't quite comprehend the magnitude of what I was going through. Talking to him was helpful, however, and he tried his best to be supportive. He understood from my shaking voice and tone of despair that I was in a great deal of turmoil over whatever it was that was going on—and suggested that maybe I should come back home to California. Since I hadn't known quite what I was doing with my life even before this had occurred, I said that I would definitely think about it. He told me to see how things went over the next day or so, and then to call back and check in—maybe he would come up with something.

I hung up and continued wandering in the direction of the apartment, struggling to get a grip on my crumbling reality, searching my brain for some conceivable way out of this bewildering situation.

My schizophrenic symptoms were increasing and multiplying by the hour. I now had flashes of light bursting throughout my consciousness as well as visibly in front of me. In addition to my feelings of intense compression, I felt simultaneously as if my soul were being pulled outwards in all directions, about to be mercilessly torn apart. The sheer force of energy moving through me felt like a freight train trying to ram its way through my soul. No matter what I did to try and alleviate the pressure, nothing made any real difference.

As I passed by a church, I decided to sit down and rest on the front steps, under the light of a single bulb shining overhead. In actuality, I sat down with an acceptance that I was going to die. I felt in that moment that I was about to somehow be obliterated into nothingness by the awesome power coursing through me and that there was nothing I could do to stop it. Nothing I had done over the past few days had led to any relief, and I was certain that I couldn't handle it for much longer. I was at the end of my rope, fully prepared at that point to let go.

I sat there staring into the darkness of the night and resigned myself to death. I expected it to overtake me at any moment. I wasn't quite sure how the final blow was going to come, but I felt certain that it was coming. I sat helplessly on those cold stone steps for a long while, waiting to die, part of me even willing death to hurry up and take me.

After fifteen or twenty minutes of just sitting there, staring out at the darkness, contemplating everything I had been through in the last few days, I began to look back over my rather unusual life. I pondered my childhood, romping through the forests of Northern California with my younger brother, chopping wood with my dad, swimming in our pond, sledding down the hill of our orchard in the occasional blanket of snow.

I thought about the many places I had been in the course of my travels over the past few years—all the people I'd met along the way whom I would miss, the wonderful memories I would cherish even in my impending unconsciousness. I felt a great sorrow overtake me for all the dreams I'd had that would never be fulfilled. I tried my best just to let them go and accept that there must be a reason for the situation in which I now found myself. Everyone had to die someday, and this must be my day.

At least I had managed to pack a lot of living into my twenty-two years. What an exciting adventure I had been lucky enough to live! How I would miss the whole experience of being human on planet Earth, hard as it was much of the time. How sad that it had to end this way, in lonely despair and confusion, when all I really wanted in life was to enjoy the simple love and beauty of the world that I knew was real, because I had experienced it plenty of times before. I was sure that I would experience that beauty again someday, if only in another lifetime. Deep down, I knew there had to be a reason for this extraordinary experience in which I now found myself immersed. Though it might not make sense at the moment, I had faith that in the end the universe was a work of perfection, and anything that might happen was part of that ultimate perfection. At some point I would understand. In the meantime, I would do my best to simply go with the flow that God seemed to have intended for me.

After a while of sitting there, contemplating, musing, and recollecting, I startled myself with a realization: not only did it appear that death wasn't going to overtake me right then, but somehow I had managed to relax into a timeless, almost peaceful reverie of sorts. As I came back to the present, I noticed that my symptoms seemed actually to have lessened slightly. A glimmer of hope was ignited in me. Was it possible that I might be able to survive this?

I noticed that, having sat there on those hard church steps for close to an hour, I was cold, tired, and getting hungry. Since it appeared that I wasn't meant to die just then—and I didn't feel like just sitting there indefinitely—I got up, walked back down the stairs, and continued in the direction of the apartment.

I felt anything but good. Though part of me had managed to accept that what I was going through must have a purpose of some kind, this in no way erased the bizarre and challenging nature of what I was experiencing. And yet, something had definitely shifted. Within myself I had resolved, for the time at least, to live.

The next day, I called my dad. He had found a cheap one-way flight from Austin back to San Francisco, and wanted to know if he should buy it for me. I told him, "Sure." Two days later—the day before Christmas—I was on my way back home.

PART 2

Digging Deep

CHAPTER 2

The few years preceding my profound Kundalini awakening were spent in Eugene, Oregon where I found myself on a spiritual roller coaster of sorts—a wild ride between revelation and desperation, and everything in between.

I moved there in the spring of 1993 from my native Northern California. I spent the first few months sharing a house with three students, doing odd jobs and yard work to pay the bills. Later, I moved out of the shared house to save on rent. I ended up living temporarily on a friend's lawn in my tent for the rest of the summer, figuring to find my own place to live as fall and the rainy season approached.

I originally moved to Eugene with the intention of going to the University of Oregon to continue my college education once I'd established Oregon residency. I'd spent two years previously going to school at the University of Alaska—another one of my spontaneous impulses that I'd chosen to follow for the adventure as much as anything else. But I never did quite make it back to school in Eugene. The intellectual pursuit simply lost its relevance for the time, as I yearned instead to understand the nature of my soul.

For reasons beyond my understanding, I found myself compelled by gut feelings to dig deep down inside my consciousness and examine whatever I might find there. In so doing, I seemed to connect with a part of myself that knew instinctively how to release my various societal repressions and heal my childhood traumas. I didn't fully comprehend at the time what I was doing in my quest for inner healing—I just did whatever seemed to help my mind break free from its self-imposed constraints—whatever helped me to understand who I really was, beneath my societal projections and restrictions. It was as if I were being dragged along by some aspect of my being that was desperate to break free, tear down the walls within, and find the greater reality that lay beyond. There was this ever-present duality within myself that I sought to resolve: extremes of elation and misery that kept yanking me around, pushing and pulling me beyond my limits of understanding, causing me to question what I perceived as reality.

I read everything I could find relating to the spiritual quest—topics ranging from death to enlightenment, lucid dreaming, astral projection, celestial dimensions, shamanism, tantra, yoga, and meditation. Shortly after moving to Eugene, I had my first out-of-body experience. I awoke in the middle of an afternoon nap to find myself facing the ceiling, a few feet away from my face. The realization that I would see my own body below if I were to turn over, however, terrified me so much that I didn't have another such experience until months later.

I found a good yoga class soon after arriving in Eugene, which helped me to ground my awakening spiritual power as well as strengthen both my body and my spirit. As I progressed with the classes, I felt a space within myself open and fill with light, increasing my depth of presence and awareness.

I spent much of my first summer there struggling with heavy, conflicting emotions, such as anger, fear, and doubt, which I presume were being stirred in me by all the potent spiritual material I was reading, as well as the effects of the yoga class. Though I didn't consciously connect to where these intense feelings were coming from, I sensed that they were related to my tumultuous teenage years and my childhood and possibly even deeper, to previous lives, or even the very birth of my soul. It seemed that I was awakening these troubling aspects of my psyche simply through my intention to confront, understand, and ultimately heal them.

A few miles outside of Eugene was an expansive, park-like arboretum, which I'd heard from some friends was a beautiful place to walk and experience the quiet of nature. One day, I decided to drive out there to check it out. I was feeling distraught and needed some time away from the bustle of the small city in which I now lived.

In the course of my walk, I happened to wander off one of the designated paths and through a meadow filled with grazing cattle. I came across a lone barn in the middle of the field, which seemed little used. I poked my head into the barn and saw that it was empty except for some hay strewn on the dusty floor. I walked inside, cleared a small circle in the hay at the center of the huge, hollow structure, and sat down in the dust to meditate.

This abandoned barn became a routine sanctuary for me over the next year-and-a-half. Whenever I was feeling lost, confused, angry, or depressed and had a few hours free, I would simply drive out to the arboretum and walk to the solitary barn to savor the silence and stillness. I would sit in the clearing I'd made in the hay and meditate, ponder the mystery of life, or sometimes express my feelings of anger and frustration in this private, non-judgmental setting. Since no one was ever around to care—other than a few contemplative cows—it was the perfect place to let out my troublesome feelings without bothering anyone.

Once I'd found some level of resolution, I would leave the empty barn and wander along the paths of the arboretum for a while, marveling at how much the world around me seemed to have changed once I'd taken the time to address what I was experiencing, rather than ignore it. My spiritual focus was instinctively becoming an attempt to acknowledge and work with so-called "negative" feelings such as anger, doubt, and fear rather than simply denying them when they arose in my life. Through my experience confronting and integrating them, I found that these were valid aspects of my own being, with the potential to be transformed if given the chance, rather than something undesirable or unacceptable to be ignored and pushed away.

In working to transform and align with these negative thoughts and emotions, I found them to be simply forms of energy. They had the power either to invigorate or depress me, depending purely on how I chose to deal with them. In listening to these aspects of myself, I found that they revealed a depth of learning and understanding that would have been inaccessible through any book or teacher; although I still had a great deal of respect for all I'd learned, spiritual and otherwise, from the experience of others. It seemed that there was a balance to be found somewhere between listening to the wisdom of others and listening to the inherent wisdom of one's own soul. I sought to find that important, often elusive balance between self and other—between my own individual consciousness, and the collective consciousness of the universe.

As that summer turned to fall, I found a steady job delivering bread around town for a local bakery. I also packed up my tent from my friend's lawn and moved into an alternative cooperative house down the street from the University of Oregon campus. I had always been interested in communal living; and besides, the rent was cheap.

I remember the first person I noticed as I was moving into the Co-op. It was a breezy day, and the fall leaves were fluttering to the ground. He was playing guitar under a tree just across the street from the large house, singing in a guttural but soulful voice. He looked at first like your typical hippie vagrant, but at second glance, maybe more like a magician. He was extremely tall and thin, had long, scraggly dark hair, a thick beard that masked half his face like a veil, dark eyes that seemed to look out from the depths of a cave, and a long, pointed nose. His name, I found out later, was Jeffrey. His presence had a certain deep, rooted power that at the time I couldn't quite grasp. He was strange and intense, and I left it at that as I busied myself with moving into my new home.

I had a single room on the top floor of the old three-story building, with just enough space to create a cozy living place with my few belongings. I was grateful to finally have my own room, after spending the previous two months in a cramped tent on my friend's lawn. I was also looking forward to living with a large group of new and interesting people.

The huge, mansion-like house had previously been a fraternity, but it had been taken over by hippies sometime during the '70s, and was now a liberal household resembling a commune. There was colorful art and poetry painted all over the walls, and plenty of philosophical commentary on the stalls of the coed bathrooms. The kitchen was the gem of the building, with beautiful artwork and graffiti covering the walls and ceiling, a number of comfy couches on which to relax, swiveling chairs, a counter to sit at during breakfast or with a cup of tea, and a grainy-sounding record player with a good selection of old records. The house was carefree but not too crazy, owing probably to the fact that all of the thirty or so residents—other than myself—were students. I'd been allowed to live there during the fall on the condition that I planned to go back to school during the spring semester.

I settled into my new home over the next few weeks as I got acquainted with the other residents and learned their unique cooperative system for cooking meals, handling assorted chores, and making the necessary household decisions. It was a diverse group of friendly and eccentric personalities. But, as I should have guessed—since it was primarily young students—most of the folks there were more intellectually focused than I was at the time. I got along well enough with everyone but, over time, I found that I didn't connect in a deeper, more spiritual way with anyone, as I had hoped I would when I moved in.

I had forgotten about Jeffrey. He didn't actually live there. In fact, it turned out that he was now homeless. But he had lived there at the communal house a few years earlier when he was going to college and so still hung out there occasionally. I had no idea that, the few times he'd been around, he had apparently been observing me, although I was soon to find that out.

CHAPTER 3

Within the first few weeks of moving into the Pearl Hill House, as it was called, I had a number of powerful spiritual experiences in rapid, unsettling succession.

The first occurred on a Thursday night at the end of my four-day workweek. The previous few days had been difficult. I'd been seeing the unpleasant reality of human suffering all around me. I had recently started the job delivering bread to local health food and grocery stores and now spent eight hours a day driving around town in a large delivery van, immersed in the aggression that people express through their automobiles.

The modern world seemed, on some level, just outright crazy. It continued to amaze me how complicated our technological lives had become in our misguided efforts to simplify them. It seemed that the real purpose of life had gotten overlooked somewhere along the way in our unending quest for progress. I wasn't altogether sure yet what that real purpose was, but I felt certain that something intangible yet fundamental to human existence was seriously lacking in the so-called "civilized" society around me.

Wherever I went around town I would observe people, since that was partly what made the job interesting. But instead of seeing only the conscious, projected selves that people were revealing, I would visualize instead their deeper spiritual and creative selves—that aspect of the soul that was yearning to break free from societal constraints, dissolve the barriers both within and without, and express itself with honesty and power.

I couldn't get this vision out of my head. It deeply distressed me that spiritual evolution, far from being a sacred aspect of our lives, was instead ridiculed or distorted by the majority of society—including most religious institutions, whose real focus seemed to be the same societal repression exhibited by the social and political powers in general. I couldn't make sense of why things had to be this way. My confusion over this matter was like a treadmill in my mind, keeping my thoughts and emotions constantly churning but never leading to any real understanding of what was actually going on in the perplexing world around me.

On that Thursday evening, I had volunteered at a small music venue in Eugene, called the WOW Hall. They played a wide assortment of music from basic rock and roll to punk, folk, reggae, techno, jazz, classical, salsa—pretty much anything or anyone that made noise. One or two nights a week I would work there for half the show, stamping hands, checking IDs, or helping set up the stage, in exchange for seeing the second half of the show for free.

After working my shift that night, I listened to the music for a little while, then left early. It was a local punk band that had apparently lost the subtle distinction between music and noise pollution. Besides, I had too much distortion going through my head already.

I drove home to the Pearl Hill House and parked near a back entrance that led up to the communal kitchen. I was immersed in my own world as I walked up the back stairs and opened the door, my troubled thoughts running in endless circles. I looked forward to a little meditation on my couch, then crawling into bed, reading for a bit, and then drifting off into the pleasant fluidity of my dreams.

As I stepped through the door, I noticed Jeffrey sitting on one of the couches in the kitchen. I hadn't actually met him yet, but for some reason—maybe I'd overheard someone else mention him—I already knew his name. And apparently, as I was about to discover, he also somehow knew mine.

As I closed the outside door and then walked across the kitchen, some part of me became aware that Jeffrey was staring intently at me. I felt deeply unnerved, as his unexpected gaze magnified all my churning thoughts and conflicting emotions. He wasn't simply getting ready to say hello. He was watching me with fixed attention, as if he'd been sitting there on that couch all evening, just waiting for me to walk through the door. I pretended not to notice his fixed gaze as I walked across the kitchen, making a comment about the cold or some trivial thing as I approached him.

The couch he was sitting on was right next to a swinging door that led out of the kitchen and into the large living room. He continued staring silently at me, boring his eyes into my soul, making me increasingly self-conscious as I neared him and the door out of the kitchen. I was trying my best to ignore the fact that something strange was going on here. Just as my hand touched the door and I was about to leave the room, he spoke. His voice was almost aggressive, like a drunk stepping directly in front of you as you walk down the sidewalk.

"What is your quest?" he asked, as if he were shouting from beyond the clouds.

I stopped and turned my head, my hand still on the door, facing him as he sat at the far end of the couch.

"Excuse me?" I said, pretending I hadn't understood him, hoping he had actually said something else—commenting on the dust, or that I needed some rest, perhaps? But how could I have not understood him, when he was asking me the very question I'd been asking myself for so long?

"What is your quest, Gabriel?" he said again with deep conviction, catching my eyes with his, reeling me in. Part of me was still trying not to acknowledge him, to persuade myself to continue on my way, and pretend that I hadn't heard his cumbersome question to begin with.

But of course, I couldn't. I was suddenly faced with a primal conflict between two opposing aspects of my being. There was a moment of timelessness in which normal reality crumbled around me, and something previously buried away became tenderly and painfully exposed. I was up against a question deep inside myself that I could no longer avoid: do I continue hiding inside my private, familiar little world, or do I leap into that great unknown abyss within, and in so doing find the greater reality—whatever that might be—that lay beyond?

But on some level I had already made my decision. The part of me that was on the lookout for a glimmer of truth—searching for something real to grab onto, courageously pushing forward into unknown circumstances, yearning for a vision of reality more sane than the one I found around myself—was clearly stronger than the scared little ego that thought it had to protect me.

I stood there for a few moments, not knowing what to say, waiting for a thought to save me from the void created by the exchange. Finally, I mumbled some nonsense...

"Uh, you caught me a little off guard."

"I know," he said. "That was the only way to reach you..."

He continued peering directly into my eyes. I felt extremely anxious, but just stood there and felt it. Some part of me desperately wanted to flee the intensity of his consciousness, gazing out at me from those dark, knowing eyes. I could tell that he sensed what I was feeling, but that it was all okay. He saw me for who I was and wasn't judging me for it, but merely perceiving and acknowledging my presence.

"You have a gift of consciousness," he said. "And you must open to feel as deeply as you can, if you wish to help heal the tremendous suffering of this planet."

I wasn't sure what to make of this statement. But I resolved to at least listen to what he had to say. Finally I took my hand from the door as he continued, the words flowing from him like a waterfall:

"The pain you have been seeing in the world around you is actually a mirror, reflecting the pain within yourself. Those who see the pain of the world are those who feel it. But you must understand that this pain you feel is not just a burden—it is also the doorway to your deepest beauty, wisdom, and strength. You must open up your own suffering from deep within yourself and allow it to express. Take a look at everything your feelings have to say. I can see that they are crying inside you to be heard—and that you are ready to listen. This is the time, now, to confront your deepest emotions and fears at the root level. Though some may say that fear and pain is only an illusion, at times it is the most honest and genuine thing we can experience—more real than any physical object."

Tears were beginning to form at the corners of my eyes as he acknowledged my inner turmoil. Before, my conflicting thoughts and emotions had just been random energy swirling around within me. Now, it was all beginning to leak out, my surface presentation shattered.

"But, if I'm such a wreck inside, what can I actually *do* that will make any real difference in the world?" I asked amidst my tears.

"You must begin, starting at the bottom rung, the movement up the ladder of the seven chakras—the energy centers in our spines that, in most of us, are deeply blocked and keep us only partially conscious, trapped in the pain of separation. With the opening of each of these blockages, you will encounter a place of darkness, a void absent of love and light. But this darkness, once you allow it to vibrate and open, can release the pain it holds and be filled with the presence of spirit, and in so doing come back to life.

"Though God may be everywhere, he is not experienced where she is not accepted. God is here right now, speaking to you through me because of your own inner call for understanding. You are beginning to realize, at this point in your life, that although physical density serves a purpose of learning, it is not really our truest state of being.

"God has slowed himself down in order to experience herself, and you and I and everything we see on this plane of existence are expressions of that experience. This Earth may seem to us to be composed of solid matter, but, as the physicists have known for some time, this isn't an entirely accurate view of things. Everything around us is in actuality light, simply slowed down and separated to create the varied density of physicality that we experience as the world around us. And yet, at the center of our beings, we and everything are still moving in perfect sync with God, at the speed of light—and we never slowed down to begin with. Our physical bodies are merely a stage in this process of evolving someday back to our natural, fluid forms of pulsing, free-flowing light. This is the great paradox of existence, what makes it all so mysterious. Our illusion of separateness from all that is, of me and you, us and them, is the yin and yang of life, the God and not-of-God that is expressed in so many ways in our universe—as day and night, man and woman, pleasure and pain, summer and winter, matter and vacuum, heaven and hell, truth and lies, movement and stillness, peace and war, life and death.

"The universe, encompassing this plane and countless others, is an infinite ocean, consisting of tiny droplets of matter, currents, waves, tides, and endless forms of beings. For anything in this ocean to think of itself as separate or independent of the ocean is a great misunderstanding. Everything comes from the ocean and goes back into the ocean. There can be no other way. There is only one ocean of life, playing with itself, laughing with itself, making love with itself endlessly in all directions—constantly moving, creating and destroying, ever-changing but always being.

"Our true self is not only that part of us which is conscious. We are like islands in the sea that, on the surface, may seem to be separate—but which deeper down reveal themselves as not only directly connected to those islands nearby, but also to the ground spreading in all directions and ultimately to everything on the planet. To identify ourselves with only that which we perceive on the surface of reality is to greatly cheat ourselves.

"Your quest is to remind yourself of this—to release your limited sense of self, to burst open all your places of inner darkness, no matter how ugly they may appear, for they are what keep you from your inherent infinity. Release the pain of your soul that keeps the clouds of your mind obscuring the pure light of your inner sun. Release the illusion that you are anything less than everything. Release the illusory belief that the world around you isn't real. The world around us is, in fact, very real. It just isn't quite what we think it is.

"Understand that your desire to know is that which will lead you towards what you seek. Desire is not the enemy, but rather the spark of life within each of us—that part of us which yearns for love and life and light. Desire for life is that which gives us all life. Desire for love has the power to manifest love into reality. Trust in your heart, and the universe will give you all that you need to live. Try to control your world with your limited sense of self, and you will continually struggle against a force far greater than you can imagine. As always, the choice is yours."

As Jeffrey finished speaking, he lowered his head slightly—his gaze still interlocked with mine—and smiled with the corners of his mouth.

I was completely silent, but reeling inside. There seemed to be nothing left to be said. At the same time, I was bursting with questions which refused to coalesce into words. I felt extremely light-headed and agitated. My mind was pulsating, as if trying to expand beyond its self-imposed limits. My ears were buzzing, and there was a knot of fire in my stomach.

"It looks like I'm getting through to you," he said.

"Yeah, I guess so…" I searched my cluttered mind for something more to say. "It all makes sense, I suppose…but how can I actually trust myself to find the truth that I seek, without going astray?"

"It will come to you," he said. "Don't worry. If you truly desire love and healing—and look and listen for it—then it will reveal itself to you, one way or another. As Jesus said, 'Seek and ye shall find.' Just open your heart, and you will be guided. And try to lose your mind for a while," he chuckled. "It's clearly not doing you much good."

He then suggested that I go to bed—I looked like I needed some rest.

I said goodnight and walked upstairs in a daze. When I got back to my room, I sat down on my tattered little couch to meditate and try to focus my scattered energy. But I couldn't resolve my inner turmoil right then. I was just too tired. Finally I crawled into bed and fell into a deep but troubled sleep.

The next day was like a dream. I could hardly believe that what had happened the previous evening was real. And yet, the fact that it *was* real was exciting, as well as a little frightening. I kept running it all through my mind, trying to fit it into the rest of the puzzle of my life.

That day I was off from work delivering bread for the bakery. I ran a few errands around town, then went to work for a man for whom I occasionally did odd jobs. I was the grunt-worker—pushing wheelbarrows of dirt down a steep, slippery hill, carrying rocks and bags of cement, pouring concrete, pounding nails. But I just couldn't keep my mind focused that day. I was scattered and clumsy. I kept dumping the wheelbarrow in the bushes halfway down the hill and spacing out while shoveling.

By the end of the long day I was exhausted and frustrated, feeling much as if I'd been tossed off a cliff—physically, emotionally, and spiritually. I drove to the bank to cash a check and almost got in an accident on the way. I drove back to the Pearl Hill House and parked my car, with a wave of relief that the trying day was finally over.

I went upstairs to my room and lay down on my bed for a few moments, reflecting on everything that had happened in the last twenty-four hours, wondering if things would get any crazier—which somehow seemed impossible and inevitable at the same time. I took a long, hot shower; then went downstairs to the kitchen to cook up something for dinner.

Jeffrey happened to be there, making something to eat for himself. I started some rice on the stove. Neither of us spoke for a while as we went about our business. Finally, he asked me how I liked living there, or something of the sort, and we carried on a conversation as if our bizarre exchange the previous night had never happened. It made me feel as if everything he'd said had actually been in my dreams, or else something out of a book I'd read—Except at one point, when he stopped talking and looked me straight in the eye for a moment, to sing a line from the Jimi Hendrix song that was playing on the record player:

"I know, I know, you'll probably scream and cry, that your little world won't let you go. But who in your measly little world are you trying to prove, that you're made out of gold, and can't be sold? Oh, are you experienced? Or have you ever been experienced? Well, I have…"

CHAPTER 4

Instead of driving to my yoga class twice a week, since it was only partway across town, I would usually bike there on my one-speed cruiser. My mountain bike had been stolen a few months earlier while I was volunteering for a show at the WOW Hall, so a friend had loaned me his spare clunker bike. It was white with flowers painted sloppily all over it, and it had big, cumbersome handlebars that curved so far down they were practically useless. The chain came off spontaneously, and every sixth pedal or so it missed a few teeth on the front gear and skipped a pedal, threatening to throw me on the pavement. But it got me around town pretty well, once I got accustomed to its quirks.

A week following my abrupt introduction to Jeffrey, a friend from yoga class, Mary, invited me to come over after class and see the house that she had just moved into with her boyfriend. After class we biked lazily across town towards her new place. When we got there she invited me in, introduced me to her boyfriend, Scott, and offered me a cup of tea. It was a great little house, very warm and cozy, just the sort of place I would have picked. The three of us talked for a little while. Then Scott turned on the TV and grabbed a large bong from beside the couch.

"You smoke?" he asked, filling the bowl with pot.

"Uh, sure..." I said, ignoring my inward hesitation, as he took a toke, and then passed me the bong.

I hesitated to smoke right then because I have a strong reaction to marijuana. Although I started smoking occasionally as a teenager, I quit a year or so later when it started making me too self-conscious and paranoid. I didn't smoke again until a few years after that, shortly after moving to Alaska to go to school. It had a similar effect on me then—though subtly different. I was able to work with its intense effects so that in some ways it actually helped me in my spiritual exploration, as long as I was in a safe and comfortable place where I could process the energies and sensations it brought up in me. Rather than numbing me to my fears and anxieties, as it apparently did for many smokers, it seemed to bring them all to my attention. It expanded my sense of awareness, bringing to full consciousness whatever inner troubles lay beneath the surface.

With this in mind, I smoked marijuana occasionally for the insight and perspective that it gave—although usually alone or else with familiar people, and in an outdoors setting away from the city. It was for this reason that I hesitated that evening, and, of course, I soon regretted not listening to myself.

Scott passed the bong around, and I took one deep hit, filling my lungs and then holding it in. But bongs have a way of increasing the effects so that it was probably equal to two or three hits from a pipe. And it must have been very good stuff because, though it generally takes a half-hour or so to peak, within just a few minutes I was feeling the effects profoundly, as a wave of intense and confusing sensory input began flooding into my consciousness.

I quickly became acutely self-conscious. Because of the yoga class that I'd just participated in plus the strange events of the previous week, I was already feeling a little raw. As the effects of the marijuana began to intensify, an overwhelming force of spiritual energy overtook me, as all my senses and perceptions became intensely magnified. My heart began to throb as if it were about to burst out of my chest. It seemed as if the air got thick and murky, the room became small and claustrophobic, and the objects around me began crowding my personal space.

My body started to feel like something separate from me, extending outward from my consciousness. At the same time, I felt as if I were trapped within it. The solidity of things around me, including my own body, seemed to melt. My presumed distinctions between the outer world and myself dissolved, as I began to lose my defining sense of who I was in relation to the world around me.

Within another twenty minutes or so, I found myself clenched in intense fear and confusion, clutching my knees against my chest as I sat on the floor, at the same time trying desperately to hide what I was experiencing from Mary and her boyfriend. At that point, I had pretty much lost all social skills, to the extent of barely being able to talk. Since I felt unable to make a dignified exit, I just sat there on the floor and watched the incessant drone of the TV— the messages of which began to take on a meaning that I had never before allowed myself to notice.

We were watching a cartoon show about a dysfunctional sub-urban family, which I had seen before and thought pretty stupid, though occasionally funny. But now I found myself reacting strongly to things that I had never really acknowledged before—sexual in-nuendoes between the family members, vague references to death, shit, and other disagreeable subjects, acts of violence passed off as humor, and the poor and shallow manner in which the people gener-ally treated one another.

Since I was raised in the woods without television, I tend to be more aware of its subconscious messages in general. But in my deep-ly expanded awareness, the insensitive, manipulative energy that it conveyed, particularly during the commercials, became magnified so that it began to feel like a form of personal invasion. I found myself horrified at the level of insensitivity, ignorance, disrespect, subtle and blatant violence, manipulation and playing on fears it portrayed—all as normal, acceptable human interactions. And this show was so-called "wholesome family entertainment."

The shallow level of awareness to which it spoke was like a stab to my heart and soul, as I realized that it was speaking to the average human being in our culture. I found myself becoming overwhelmed with sorrow and grief that this lack of reverence for life to some extent represented the basic level of consciousness encircling our planet. Though I had always had a sense that something was terribly wrong in our world, the reality now hit me deep in my being of how horribly screwed up modern-day human society is. Although we see evidence of this every day on the evening news in terms of the terrible things that people do to one another, I had never quite seen how this dark reality pervaded our society in other, subtler ways. A veil of illusion was stripped from my eyes, and what I now saw was almost more than I could handle.

As I sat there shaking and clutching my knees, overwhelmed and cracking apart with these various realizations and revelations, to make things worse, I suddenly felt as if I were about to fully separate from my body somehow. Scott had poured me a glass of water at one point, sensing that I was having something of a bad high. But I found myself unable to drink the water, due to an altered view of myself in relation to both the water and the glass. Trying to put the glass up to my mouth, I realized that there was some strange, subtle separation between my consciousness and my physical body. I experienced myself not as simply moving the glass with my hand to my mouth, but as commanding my body to move itself. Though I was obviously connected to my body somehow, I wasn't really "in it" in quite the way that I had always thought I was. It felt almost as if that which I called "I" was actually a command center somewhere within my mind, centered in my head, that was ordering my body to perform the tasks that it so desired.

It was with this disconcerting realization that I almost totally lost control. I felt as if I were about to lift up and out of my body somehow, as everything in the room appeared to shift momentarily into another dimension of perception. It was fascinating for an instant, but far more frightening. My body went through a spasm as I pulled myself back down into it, fearing that, for all I knew, I just might die, or else black out, if I didn't get a grip on my experience. Although I'd never heard of someone overdosing on marijuana, I certainly didn't want to be the first. I held tightly onto myself, determined not to let go, clutching my knees as if they were a shred of rope dangling over a deep precipice of darkness within my own consciousness.

Finally, I decided that I had to leave. I seemed to be coming down slightly and was able to find my daypack, put on my shoes, and say goodnight to Scott and Mary without creating too much of a scene. Although they apparently sensed that I hadn't been feeling so well, they didn't seem to make too much of it. I stumbled out into the night, found my bicycle leaning against a nearby bush, tried to ride it and realized that I couldn't. Instead I walked with it down a side street towards the comfort and security of my room at the Co-op, thanking the guiding spirits for my having apparently survived intact the revealing but terrifying drug trip I'd just been through.

CHAPTER 5

A few weeks later, I experienced yet another dramatic spiritual development, though this one was less disconcerting than
those of the previous weeks. It was again one of my days off,
and all day I had been feeling lousy; though what I was actually feeling
I couldn't quite identify. It was simply an indescribable psychological
heaviness that stayed with me through the day, weighing me down as
I tried to take care of my chores and go about other assorted business.

As the day wore on, this inner heaviness became more and more
intense. I became incredibly tired, and my limbs began to feel almost
numb. I had a terrible headache and upset stomach and felt extremely anxious and scattered. It was as if all of my internal energy channels were clogged up, leaving me feeling…nothing…lifeless. I knew
that somehow I needed to break through and release whatever inner
blockages were keeping my energy level dragged down, but I was at
a loss as to what to do that might help.

Later that evening, I went upstairs to my room to meditate and try
to clear my heavy state of mind. Although meditation was helpful
for me at times, this time I was unable to sort it out simply through
the focus of my mind. I decided just to lie down on my back on my
bed and allow myself to both observe and experience everything that
I was feeling—to fully merge with the blockages rather than seek
ways to escape or deny them. It felt surprisingly good just to relax
into all the subtle feelings going through my mind and body, to surrender to the experience and give it my full attention, as apparently
negative as they were.

I lay there for perhaps an hour, unmoving, with eyes closed. By doing this, I was eventually able to penetrate the dense energy and find

what felt like my center in the midst of it all—a place of calm within the storm that I could now clearly sense amidst all the discord.

As I lay there on my back becoming more and more centered and grounded, it was as if I passed through the blocked energy and found myself somehow underneath it. I could feel all the trapped energy hovering just above my body, as if it were ready to break away and fly free. I became so relaxed that I almost forgot for the time being that I had a body at all. It felt as if I were simply hovering in space, with the presence of this blocked energy vibrating subtly above me.

As I let go of the last bit of tension, this energy quite suddenly burst up and away from me. At the same time, my entire body began to vibrate. I allowed it to do so, despite how strange it seemed, because it felt great. As I let go entirely to the flowing energy, my body vibrated more and more, shaking and contorting on the bed as the energy blockages flowed out and through me.

Eventually I slowed down and stopped, still lying on my back and breathing heavily, my heart almost pounding out of my chest. Once I'd regained my breath, I continued the bodily vibrating for probably ten or fifteen minutes, until there seemed to be no blocked energy left to be released. Then I turned onto my side and just lay there, experiencing the joy and lightness of pure energy flowing freely through me.

I couldn't remember the last time that I'd felt so centered, calm, relaxed, open, and totally present. I got up and went to take a long shower, and then went back to my room and sat on my couch for a while. There was absolutely nothing that I needed in that moment. Nothing to do, nowhere to go. I just sat and looked around me at the objects in my room, noticing how dramatically my perception had shifted, once again, in spite of the fact that nothing outwardly had actually changed. It was perfectly clear to me in that moment what happiness was: just being truly alive, basking in the pure presence of spirit. That is all there is to it; it's so simple.

This method of bodily vibration became a powerful tool along my spiritual path over the next few years. Due to the energy openings that I had facilitated earlier through emotional expression, yoga, meditation, and spiritual reading, I was beginning to connect more deeply with the many different energetic layers of my conscious— and previously unconscious—spiritual being. In so doing, I was also contacting deeper, more subtle and yet more powerful inner block- ages. This dense, stuck energy needed release in a very simple and direct, yet deeply effective way. This process of bodily vibrating seemed to be just what was needed to get the energy really moving. Although I couldn't comprehend it at the time, I believe that what I was really doing with all of this energy movement was mining the depths of my consciousness, to get to the real energy source at the center of it all—the Kundalini fire.

CHAPTER 6

It was around this same time that I had my second spontaneous out-of-body experience. My first interest in the phenomenon had come about a year or so earlier, when I came across Robert A. Monroe's book *Journeys Out of the Body*. I'd read it enthusiastically and followed his instructions for achieving the out-of-body state, though without success—until it happened unexpectedly six months later, as previously mentioned.

Shortly after I moved to Eugene, I was lying in bed one evening, listening to some soothing music after a long day doing yard work. I relaxed and started dozing off. I'm not sure if I ever actually fell into real sleep, though I definitely went through some kind of semi-conscious state. Sometime after I thought that I had fallen asleep, I abruptly woke up—or at least, I became suddenly, acutely conscious.

I found myself disoriented, trying to figure out which way I was facing, puzzled that I had apparently ended up facing the wall at the head of the bed. Then I realized that, in fact, I was facing not the wall but the ceiling, which was about two feet from my face.

I went through a quick state of shock and confusion as it hit me that I was actually out of my body. I then went through another rush—of excitement—as I felt a sense of defiant success for having accomplished what I had been attempting six months earlier. And then the reality struck me that if I were to somehow turn over, I would see my own body lying on the bed below me.

This thought made me so uncomfortable that I immediately willed myself back into my body and woke up—this time for real—with a sense of relief at being back in my body and in the "real" world.

But I was also inspired by my accomplishment and was left feeling deeply, sublimely relaxed by the experience. It felt as if I had, in some sense, bathed my soul—perhaps because contacting the metaphysical realms in some regard, however briefly, had awakened a remembrance of some other spiritual state of being.

Several months after this event and a few weeks following the above-mentioned series of unsettling experiences, I began to experience a peculiar state just before I fell asleep. As I began to fall asleep, at some point I would experience a strange, indescribable sensation—something like a veil shrouding my soul being lifted, or perhaps a doorway within my mind somewhere being opened.

After falling asleep on one of these nights, I abruptly became conscious—in a manner similar to the previous experience—and found myself hovering above the floor, face down, on the far side of my room. I was simultaneously surprised, scared, and yet oddly calm. I tried to stay present with the experience for a few moments, attempting to move around a little, but my fear of this unfamiliar state was just too much and I was suddenly back in my bed, opening my eyes to normal wakefulness.

This began to happen fairly frequently. On a few occasions, I was even conscious as I slipped out of my body. The experience of going out-of-body could be compared to that of taking off one's clothes, but with an even deeper sensation of spiritual nakedness quite beyond description. It felt as if I were connecting with long lost memories of primal existence, plugging in a whole new set of inner spiritual connections that tingled through me with electrifying energy. I felt somehow far more intensely alive; so much so that it was overwhelming. I experienced a profound sense of freedom, as I imagined I'd feel if I were flying through the air, soaring through the clouds, far above mountains, valleys, rivers, and other beings, seeing everything from a distant and expansive perspective. And as I understood it, based on the reading I'd done, I could have even experienced this directly, if I could have figured out how to actually leave the room. But the experience, though thrilling to some extent, was still far too intense for me to handle for much longer than just a few moments. My fear always overpowered my desire to stay present with it, and I quickly found myself back in my body, engulfed in awe at what had just taken place.

After a few weeks of this occurring a few times a week, I started to get pretty spaced out, to say the least. Despite my intense curiosity to discover more, I realized that I had to discontinue my exploration of the out-of-body state, at least for the time. There were too many other bizarre things happening in my life, and I knew that it wasn't in my best interest right then to experiment with such a powerful and otherworldly phenomenon. Staying grounded was never one of my strong points and this wasn't helping. I simply willed myself to stop, refusing to relax into the strange states I had been experiencing as I fell asleep. After a week or two I no longer slipped out of my body at night, and my desire to experience such a state again pretty much disappeared. I had gotten a real taste of that which I had read about, and that was enough.

CHAPTER 7

Over the next few months, my life went through many changes. Spring was now approaching, and I sold my old station wagon to buy an even older pickup truck with a camper shell for summer camping and road trips.

Also, I decided to move out of the busy sensory and social atmosphere of the Pearl Hill household to get some much-needed peace and quiet. Besides, I'd decided to put off school for another semester, so I no longer had the choice to stay there anyway. My friend Matt (whose lawn I had lived on the previous summer) and his girlfriend Sharon had rented a new place together, a little house with an extra room. They invited me to stay with them while I was looking for another place to live. Though it was a funky house, pretty run down and next to a busy street, the rent was cheap, and it would be a welcome change from the communal responsibilities and constant activity of the Pearl Hill House. Plus, it would give me the chance to spend some time with Matt and Sharon.

I moved into their place at the end of January and ended up living with them for a couple of months. Eventually, I found another room, in a house with three like-minded housemates. Soon afterwards I quit my early-morning job delivering bread and got another job delivering pizza in the evenings. I progressed with my yoga and meditation and continued to make regular trips out to the barn at the arboretum, or else to some nearby hot springs or river swimming spots, to get out of town and connect with nature. I also continued my process of bodily vibrating, releasing ever-more deepening layers of blocked and frozen energy, and in so doing bringing light into parts of myself previously shrouded in darkness.

I still saw Jeffrey around town every once in a while. If I happened to be on foot or on my bike, then I would always stop and talk with him. He was the one person in Eugene that I could connect with on a truly deep and real level—with whom I could wholeheartedly share my spiritual challenges and experiences of personal growth. He walked a path similar to my own, so he could understand my dilemmas like no one else in my life at the time. It always gave me a sense of reassurance and grounding to connect with him and be reminded that I wasn't entirely alone on this ongoing, bewildering spiritual path.

That summer brought many adventures. One was that my younger brother, Christo, came up from school in California for summer break. I got him a job at the pizza parlor where I was now working, and he ended up moving into Matt and Sharon's place for the summer, into the same spare bedroom where I had previously been staying.

Shortly after Christo rolled into town, he and I, along with my yoga instructor John and three other people from yoga class, took off for a two-week summer vacation, and headed for the 1994 annual Rainbow Gathering festival, in western Wyoming that year. I'd been to one such event the previous summer, and John had been to several.

The six of us left Eugene late morning near the end of June in two pickup trucks: John's and mine. We drove all that day through the Oregon desert. We spent the first night at a rest stop along the way. The next day, we drove across Idaho, to a small town on the Wyoming border. A few miles into Wyoming, we eventually found the narrow Forest Service road that led into National Forest. It turned after a few miles from pavement to gravel and then to dust, as the evening sun was fading below the horizon.

As seems to be the tradition on the way to Rainbow Gatherings, three hours and only thirty miles later, we were thoroughly lost. After passing other hippie-laden vehicles in the dark, also lost, we finally stopped at a pull-off to spend that night camped by the side of the road. We made a campfire to cook dinner and then lay out our sleeping bags on the ground under the expansive Wyoming sky.

The next morning, we came across another carload of people—with better directions than our own—and we followed them, after several more winding, dusty miles, to the Welcome Home parking lot. We parked our trucks in a huge clearing filled with row after row of vehicles. From there, we packed up our backpacks, drums, shovel and water containers, and hiked the three miles down a path to the main circle meadow, with many a "Welcome home!" along the way from folks passing by. We stopped to rest in the huge main meadow, at a large circle of folks forming there for a late breakfast of oatmeal and pancakes with honey.

We joined the circle for a free and delicious breakfast (it's indeed true that everything tastes better in the woods) as well as some friendly conversation with like-minded folks. Afterwards we hefted our belongings onto our backs, once again, for the final push, and hiked into the woods to find a good campsite. Soon enough we found an excellent spot, amidst a large grove of trees in the center of another large meadow, a short stroll through the woods from the circle we'd just attended at the main meadow.

The annual national Rainbow Gathering is an event like no other. It is a free-form festival held in one of America's many National Forests, with as many as 30,000 people attending. It is a month-long ceremony, imbued with deep primal energy, emotion, spirituality, and love. But, unlike many gatherings of alternative-living folks these days, such as bluegrass festivals, hemp fests, farmer's markets, reggae festivals, or renaissance fairs—in which the people gather around a particular band or theme—most people go to a Rainbow Gathering for the sole purpose of hanging out together. It is essentially a huge family reunion, of many different sorts of people, who come together to celebrate in a myriad of different ways. It quickly takes on the feeling of a small village spread throughout the forest.

Now, in case you're horrified at how this might impact the land, I should mention that, despite what might sound like chaos, there is actually a fair amount of organization to the event. Although no one is paid—since it is entirely free—hundreds of people, many of them older hippie veterans, volunteer their time and energy long before the gathering begins to prepare the site for the thousands of people who will gather for the central week of festivities.

There is always a vast meadow that acts as the center of the gathering, where circle is called and meals served. Food is prepared by dozens of volunteer kitchens that spring up throughout the forest, some of them a mile or more from main circle. Food supplies are either donated or else paid for by money collected in the "magic hat," which is passed around the circle at each evening meal.

If a person should happen to miss breakfast or dinner or is hungry in the middle of the day or any time of night, they can be sure of finding something to eat, a cup of coffee or tea, cookies, popcorn or tobacco at one of the many kitchens, down one of the narrow trails leading into the woods—built from downed branches, twine and plastic tarps by groups of grubby, scraggly, hairy, sweaty, smoky-faced, smiling, arguing, laughing, ragged-clothed, dreadlocked, beaded, necklaced, nose-ringed, tattooed, and half or completely naked men and women, young and old; dogs and kids frolicking nearby, folks playing drums, flutes, guitars and didgeridoos around crackling fires, smoking marijuana and rolling tobacco, telling stories and jokes, singing songs, hugging, giving massages, having philosophical discussions and arguments, sharing love, ideas and emotion of all kinds. The kitchens have names like Everybody's Kitchen, Turtle Soup, Bliss, Popcorn Palace, Jah Love, Granola Funk, Om Chapati, Aloha Camp, Pizza Pete's, Sunshine Camp, Northwest Tribes, Whatever Kitchen and Graceland Tea Mansion.

But the food is only one aspect of the gathering. Go farther down that same trail, cross a stream, up a hill to another, smaller meadow, and you'll find a group of naked men and women standing quietly around another fire, waiting for the coals to heat the rocks for a sweat lodge ceremony. At the far end of main meadow is a silent teepee, set aside for group meditation. There's also Kid Village—devoted entirely to children and their families—with naturally crafted jungle gyms and rope-swings. CALM, the Center for Alternative Living Medicine, is a healing camp for both physical and mental ailments. Krishna Camp has ongoing chanting and dancing, and the best food in town. Yoga classes can be found at various camps or in the main meadow. And a trading circle forms what could be termed "downtown Rainbow." Although exchanging money in a National Forest is illegal, there are no limits on trading goods, and some come primarily for this part of the gathering.

As night falls, you might stumble across a story-telling tent, a talent show complete with disco ball, folks making music around small fires, or pounding drums circling a raging campfire in the main meadow, echoing the heartbeat of the people throughout the forest.

One of the beautiful—and sometimes tragic—things about the Rainbow Gatherings is that almost every type of person can be found there. You'll see folks of every age, ethnic and religious group; from yuppies to hippies, Hell's Angels to faerie folk (sometimes even with wings), gutter punks and Native American shamans, old crones and ex-cons.

Although alcohol isn't allowed in the main gathering area, at the edge of the gathering somewhere near the parking area can be found A-Camp (Alcohol Camp) where they drink beer, eat red meat, do hardcore drugs, and occasionally get into fist fights, or worse. A-camp can at times be something of an antithesis to the more pure and peaceful focus of the Rainbow Gathering itself. Every few years, it seems, there's a reported rape or assault at the gathering—usually occurring in A-Camp. Because, unfortunately, this ugliness is a harsh reality of human existence and society anywhere, it is an anticipated (although, of course, not at all supported or accepted) aspect of the all-encompassing humanity of the gatherings.

As the name implies, these festivals in the woods are meant to include all colors of the proverbial rainbow—regardless of a person's race, culture, religion, politics, societal status, dress, sexuality, or whatever other means people might choose to delineate themselves.

The image of the rainbow, as accepted by many spiritual disciplines, corresponds to the different chakras that ascend up our spines, from red at the root to purple at the crown. Each color represents a different energy, which has something different and unique to offer. And each person's aura has an emphasis on a different chakra. Life would be pretty dull if we were all exactly the same and if all that existed was white light. If this were the case, then there would of course be no differentiation between anything at all, and thus no individual experience. Different colors and energies, it seems, are what make existence in our world possible—not to mention interesting. This belief is the underlying philosophy of the Rainbow Gatherings: for all the different colors and myriad shades of the rainbow of humanity to be welcomed and represented.

Although we stayed at the Rainbow Gathering for ten amazing days, the most profound experience for many, including myself, came just a few days after we'd arrived. The forest was extremely dry that summer. There had been a few reports of mysterious, unconfined fires in the first few days of the gathering, which had quickly been discovered and put out. Everyone was warned of the potential fire danger, and people were keeping their eyes wide open for unsupervised fires.

I was sitting at a small council meeting in main meadow, discussing this very issue of fire safety, when, from the far side of the meadow came urgent, desperate shouts of "Fire!! Fire!!!"

The group of us got up from where we were seated in the grass and rushed in the direction of the voice coming through the forest. We could already see smoke rising from above the trees. As we crossed the wide meadow and approached the woods, a number of people came rushing towards us. One of them was yelling, "It's too late! It's totally out of control! Move back! There's nothing we can do about it right now…we've got to get out of here!"

We could see dark smoke beginning to billow high above the trees, coming apparently from a ways back in the forest. But the wind was blowing towards us and, judging by the increasingly dark, reddish plumes of smoke, the fire was growing rapidly. We expected it to come bursting out into the meadow at any time.

We all moved back towards the center of the meadow, not yet ready to concede actually leaving the area for good. People were coming out of the trees from all directions to gather in the clearing of the main meadow. Many were shouting various commands of what to do. All of them sounded as if they knew for certain what needed to be done to deal with the sudden crisis at hand.

"Start packing up your belongings! The only thing we can do is leave, before the whole forest burns down!!" one guy was yelling.

"No, we've got to start a bucket brigade if we want to save our home!" Another man was shouting desperately. "Don't leave if you love the forest!"

Still others were trying to calm people down, saying that we should just stay in the meadow where it was safer than in the trees, until we had better instructions as to what to do and how bad the situation really was. I followed this advice, which sounded the most reasonable, keeping my eyes open for John and my brother Christo, who were elsewhere at the gathering that day. I stayed in the meadow with many others, marveling at the event taking place before my eyes, and the different ways in which people were reacting to the crisis.

There was soon a steady file of people leaving the gathering with their belongings. Many more were gathering in the meadow to watch in awe of the billowing smoke filling the sky. There were also lone people sitting in the grass meditating, and small groups praying and holding hands, in stark contrast to those running around, shouting commands to one another, some of whom even had walkie-talkies to shout into. It was good to know that there was at least a hint of modern technology here to help us out, since we were clearly in a situation over most of our hippie heads.

A huge circle of confused and concerned, yet energized people was amassing in the meadow. In the center of the circle, a large pile of white five-gallon buckets was forming. Some people were filling them in the creek and bringing them back to the circle, gearing up to some-how combat the fire. At one point we were informed, by someone who sounded fairly authoritative, that the Forest Service was coming in with a bomber to drop some kind of chemical onto the fire, and that we had to be prepared, in case we were hit by any of the stray powder drifting in the wind. Those of us in the circle were being advised to cover our faces with something to filter out both the impending chem-icals and the smoke, and then squat down with our heads between our legs, our hands covering our necks. Why exactly we needed to do all this was never made fully clear. It seemed that simply covering one's face with a bandanna and then keeping one's eyes open would do the trick for the time being, which was what I did.

After twenty or thirty more minutes of this progressing pandemo-nium and no sign of the bomber, I realized that we weren't all going to be bombed quite yet and, in the meantime, I wanted to get some pictures of the momentous event taking place.

I ran back to our campsite (fortunately in the opposite direction of the fire), grabbed my camera and daypack from my tent, and then hurried back to the meadow and started discreetly taking photos, keeping my bandanna on and one eye open. Although the smoke filling the sky above the forest was steadily increasing, along with the sounds and smells of burning trees, the fire seemed to still be a ways back in the forest in an area where, fortunately, there were few people camped. It was not yet, at least, bursting forth to burn every-thing down around us.

Eventually, I heard another report of a bomber coming in. We all waited in anticipation. A short time later, sure enough, a plane was spotted in the distance, coming over the trees towards us and headed straight for the dark cloud of smoke. It roared overhead, and dropped a huge load of orange powder into the trees above the fire. A little while later, yet another bomber roared overhead and dropped its load into the billowing smoke. A huge cheer erupted from all of us.

However, we soon heard unfortunate news: both planes had actu-ally missed the fire with their loads. And there would be no more help from the Forest Service, due to lack of personnel and resources. Apparently, there were major forest fires all over the West that summer, and ours was one of the small ones by comparison.

Just then—while I was feeling a great wave of helplessness amidst the circle where I was sitting—a man came running out of the woods nearby, yelling, "Come on! We're starting a bucket brigade right now, and we need as many people to help out as possible!"

At the same time, a man on a horse was trying to argue with him, "No, it's too dangerous…we can't go back in there, the fire could overtake us at any minute."

"It's okay," said the other guy. "I've been back in there already, and the fire is somehow dying down on its own. But we need people to help put it out, before it starts to blaze again."

I immediately jumped up, ready to take some action, tired of sitting around helplessly all afternoon. I ran off into the woods, along with many other folks, in the direction he had indicated, to find out how we could help out.

A bucket brigade was indeed forming at the creek. There was already a long line leading from the creek up the hill in the general direction of the fire. I took my place in it and began alternately handing heavy, full buckets of water up the line, and then tossing the empty ones back down the hill towards the creek.

As more and more people joined the brigade at the bottom, we were all moved farther up the hill until I could see wisps of smoke coming through the trees. I wet my bandanna once again and tied it back around my face and throat as I moved deeper into the woods, eventually coming to charred trees and ground, and shoots of smoke coming out of the dirt.

The scene in the forest nearest the fire was a madhouse. People were scattered all over the place carrying the full buckets of water right up to the charred and smoking trees, a few of which were still on fire, to varying degrees. The previously raging flames had clearly died down a great deal. Apparently the wind had suddenly changed directions, forcing the fire back onto itself, so that most of its available fuel had already been exhausted. But the effects of those few hours of burning had left a charred, though still standing, forest in its wake.

There were a number of people with chainsaws roaring, cutting down dangerously hanging limbs and trees, as well as people hauling smoking logs and branches from the greener part of the forest, back into the part that had mostly burned. Some had shovels and were digging into the smoking ground to expose and douse burning roots. People were yelling back and forth through the trees for more water, shovels, and people to help. Upon someone's suggestion I started taking buckets of water back into the green part of the forest looking for smoke coming up through the ground. This indicated root fires that had the potential to start the forest fire all over again.

The bucket brigades went on for hours and hours, through the rest of the day and into the evening. I eventually discovered that there were other lines of people passing buckets, coming up from another creek in a different part of the forest and decided to follow it down to the beginning to see if they needed more help. In the process I happened across Jeffrey there, filling buckets in the creek.

"Hey, welcome to the party!" he said, as he looked up and saw me. I had actually known that he was going to be at the gathering and had seen him there earlier but hadn't had the chance to hang out and talk with him at all. I joined in the line next to him, happy to see a familiar face, and continued helping get the filled buckets out of the creek, then handing them up to the next person in line.

Evening was descending into darkness, and we were all beginning to slow down considerably, our arms, bodies and minds way beyond exhaustion. Finally, we heard the news making its way down the line: the fire was out, and we could stop. But we continued, not wanting to stop until we were absolutely sure. A few minutes later, we heard someone yell down with an air of certainty from the top of the hill:

"Stop! Stop filling buckets! The fire is completely out!!"

A huge wave of relief and exhaustion passed through us all—as well as amazement that we had actually succeeded in putting out the fire without any outside help. The bucket brigade came to an abrupt halt, as a cheer went up through the line, and we all joined in, hollering into the forest our delight at having accomplished what had seemed an impossible task earlier in the day.

Though slightly smaller than before, the Rainbow Gathering continued on following the crisis of the fire. Many actually felt it to be a powerful initiation and cleansing of sorts, which served to strengthen and purify the energy of the gathering.

A week later, it was nearing the end of the Rainbow Gathering. I was sitting in a circle waiting for John to begin our routine morning yoga session in the main meadow, when a tall, young woman with long, dark hair happened to walk by our little group. One of the young men around the circle spoke up as she passed by: "Hey there, you want to join us for a yoga session? We're just getting started…"

"Well, I was actually headed down to the solar showers…" she said. "But sure, I might as well; I could use a little exercise to start my day. I guess I can always take my shower afterwards…"

"What's your name?" asked the same fellow who had invited her, as she came to join the yoga circle.

"Amy," she said, as she sat down next to me, smiling and bringing her legs into cross-legged position. John then brought his hands together at his heart in prayer position, and we all did the same, closing our eyes and taking a deep breath, letting out a group *Om* to begin the session, as the sun shone down upon our dusty faces.

Later that day, my brother and I helped out in one of the many kitchens preparing food for dinner where Amy happened to be working. Christo and I ended up talking with her and her friend Lisa, while we all cut potatoes and other veggies together. She was three years younger than myself, from Austin, Texas, and she and Lisa were on a wild summer road trip together, which had unexpectedly brought them here, to their first Rainbow Gathering. They hadn't even heard of the event until a week or so earlier, when they'd picked up a hitchhiker who was going there and decided to check it out.

Amy and Lisa weren't quite sure where they were going onwards from there. Amy had an aunt in Portland, Oregon, whom she was thinking of visiting. I mentioned that I was living in nearby Eugene and she suggested maybe they could stop by and say hello, if they happened to pass through the area sometime later.

A few days later, as we were sadly taking down our tents and packing up our belongings to leave the gathering and head back home, Christo said, "Hey, I should give those two girls our phone number before we go." I had pretty much forgotten about Amy and Lisa by then, considering our fairly brief encounter. "Sure," I said. "If you want to, go ahead and we'll wait here for you."

He ran off to the kitchen where we'd worked with them a few days before, hoping they might be there. Soon he came back, saying that they'd said goodbye, and hoped to see us in Eugene at some point. Little could I have realized at the time the effect that my brother's simple action would have on the future course of my life.

CHAPTER 8

Bizarre, unexpected things took place around me following the Rainbow Gathering. I found myself caught up in a maelstrom of unanticipated events that left me confused and shaken and that, once again, managed to blow me wide open. I tried to get back into my usual routine of working at the pizza joint, living in the city in a house with three other people, and making occasional trips out of town to find some silence and connect with the peace and quiet of nature. But something that I couldn't quite identify or figure out seemed out of place. The inner peace that I sought always managed to elude me. My spiritual quest seemed to have no eventual resolution, like some kind of cruel cosmic hoax, a carrot at the end of a stick leading me always in some inexplicable direction.

Late one evening after work, a couple of weeks after returning from the Rainbow Gathering, I got a call from Amy and Lisa. They were in town right at that moment and thinking of heading up to nearby Cougar hot springs for a few days. They wanted to know if my brother and I would like to come along. I wasn't sure exactly what my schedule was the next few days, but I invited them to come over and at least crash at my place for the night. They said "sure," they were actually hoping that I might make such an offer—they'd be right over.

They soon arrived at my door, and I gave them both big rainbow hugs. Besides the fact that they were beautiful young women, I was happy just to see someone else from the Rainbow Gathering, since it was beginning to fade into a distant, hazy memory, more like a dream than something I'd recently experienced. Although we hadn't spent all that much time together there, just having the experience in common gave us an instant bond, an openness that I didn't share even with my housemates of the last few months. Although my housemates were all young, friendly, creative people with whom I got along well, there was something magical about the Rainbow Gatherings that opened up a long dormant part of the soul, so that virtual strangers might become good friends in a matter of days or even hours.

One way or another, Amy and I ended up alone in my room that night, talking into the early hours. Around three or four in the morning, we finally decided that we'd better get some sleep. She got up out of the lounge chair next to my bed to leave, and I got up from my bed, where I had been lying on my side, to give her a hug. We embraced one another, as love flowed between us like a warm, comforting breeze. We had wanted to touch one another all night, but hadn't found the opportunity until now. We just stood there holding each other, eyes closed, feeling the energy flow freely between us, squeezing each other softly, caressing one another's backs with our hands, feeling the soft touch of our embracing bodies.

Eventually, I motioned her to the bed, and we pulled back the covers and crawled under the warm blankets. We resumed our embrace, kissing each other softly. Finally we fell asleep, still holding each other close.

We awoke late the next morning to Lisa knocking on the door, having reasoned that we must be in there together.

"Wake up, you sleepyheads! Let's go to the springs!"

As it turned out, I had the next two days off, although, to his frustration, my brother had to work the next few nights at the pizza parlor, so he wasn't able to join us. Amy, Lisa, and I left town that morning. I followed the two of them in my Datsun pickup truck out to the hot springs, about forty miles east of Eugene. We camped together at a free campground a couple of miles down the road from the springs.

Amy and I spent the next couple of days in the general vicinity of the hot springs, sharing a lot of affectionate time together. When I had to head back to Eugene to go to work, she decided to come hang out with me for a little longer. Lisa kept the car they were road-tripping in and continued camping with some other friends of theirs. Amy and I then drove back into town, and she stayed at my place. We spent the next few days hanging out a lot—walking around town, talking, playing games, napping and cuddling, before I went to work in the evenings.

A few days later, Lisa came back into town to pick Amy up and, sadly, I hugged them both goodbye, as they headed back north to Portland. Their plan was to stay with Amy's aunt in Portland for a while, get jobs, make a little money, and then continue their road trip full circle back to Texas. I hoped they would stay there for a while, so that I could come up and visit them in Portland, or else they could come down to Eugene—whatever would give Amy and me the chance to spend more time together.

About a week after Amy and Lisa went up to Portland, I started a five-day fast. I felt the need for an internal cleansing, both physically and mentally. I stopped eating solid foods and drank only water and juice (and lots of it) for the next five days. I only worked delivering pizza two evenings out of those five days, so I was able to spend most of the time at home, sleeping, reading, writing in my journal, going for short walks, and generally trying to stay calm and centered. Perhaps subconsciously I was preparing myself for changes that I sensed lay ahead.

At the time that I was doing this fast, Julia, the sister of a friend of one of my housemates, was staying at our house. She had just moved to Oregon from the East Coast after breaking up with her boyfriend. She needed somewhere to crash for a few weeks while looking for her own place and starting a new life for herself in Oregon. This didn't bother me at all, considering that I'd stayed with friends myself for a while when I'd first moved to Eugene, so I could relate. Besides, there were always people coming and going, with the friends and family of four different people stopping by. It was a roomy house, and Julia was a kind enough person, although I did notice that she seemed a little distant and melancholy at times. What *was* quite unnerving, however, was that over the next few days, Julia went completely crazy.

We all noticed that she seemed to be getting more and more distant each day, but we were all rather distracted by our own lives and didn't make too much of it at first. It was when she started wandering around the house naked, muttering and singing to herself and unable to carry on a normal conversation with anyone, that we all realized something was definitely way out of the ordinary.

This was on a Friday, the final day of my challenging fast as well as the day that Amy called with an unusual personal scenario of her own. Her friend Lisa, tired of looking for a job and not finding one, had left Portland a few days before with some other folks they'd met at the Rainbow Gathering, and headed down to Santa Cruz, California. Amy had stayed behind in Portland because she'd already found a part-time job. Her plan was to meet up with Lisa after she'd made a little money. But Lisa called only a few days after leaving to say that the people she'd driven down to California with were turning into freaks, she hated Santa Cruz, and wanted to drive back home to Texas right away. Amy decided to quit her job right away since she had the car. She was headed out the door right at that minute, to drive down to Santa Cruz and rescue Lisa.

I was heartbroken at her sudden departure—even more so because she didn't seem terribly concerned about leaving behind our blossoming relationship. I understood that her concern was for her long-time friend and that she'd only known me for a few weeks. But it still hurt, because I realized that I'd made more of the relationship than it seemed it really was. But, at least, she said that she could spend that night with me in Eugene before continuing south down Interstate-5 the next morning.

She showed up at my house late that evening, to find the weird situation that I'd forgotten to mention over the phone. Julia was wandering around the house naked, singing to herself, carrying on conversations with nobody, and generally acting like a crazy person; while the rest of us were trying to go about the house as usual, not knowing what else to do. I had pretty much disconnected from the situation, feeling too overwhelmed myself after the past five days of fasting to deal with it. Julia's sister had been alerted to the situation, and we were all hoping she would come up with a solution sometime soon.

Amy and I stayed on the front porch late into the night, talking and holding one another, though it was clear that I was less in her heart now than when she'd stayed with me a few weeks before. Her mind was clearly occupied with concern for her friend Lisa.

She stayed over that night and then left early the next morning. I was sad to see her go. Her unexpected presence a few weeks before had been a blessing, in what was beginning to feel now like my empty and hollow life. I hadn't managed to find a steady girlfriend in the year-and-a-half I'd been in Eugene, and I realized then how much I wanted to be in a partnership with a woman, sharing together my path of adventure, exploration, and learning. Before she left, Amy invited me to come to Texas and visit her sometime. It was shortly afterwards that I started thinking seriously about leaving Eugene for good.

Later that day, Julia's sister finally called the local social services clinic, to come pick her up and take her to a psychiatric facility. She was acting increasingly hostile towards the men in the house and wouldn't talk clearly even to her own sister, who was extremely apologetic to us all but didn't know how to help her. I was gone when they came over to get her and relieved when I returned to find the drama finally over.

There was something about this particular weekend that attracted all manner of random, unsettling circumstances. In addition to the incident with Julia, and Amy's rushing through with her own frantic situation, one of our ex-housemates, who had moved up to Portland a month earlier, came by the next day to get his couch and dining room table, which we all were using. Suddenly we had nowhere to sit in the living room and no table to eat on. And just a few days after Amy left, I got a $150 traffic ticket for running a red light while working one evening. My brake pads had been screeching lately from undue wear. When I came speeding towards the intersection, I'd decided to go for it rather than slam on my squeaky brakes, even though the light was turning from yellow to red. A friendly female cop was at the front of on-coming traffic to catch me in the act, though not quite friendly enough to let me off, even though I explained that I would be getting my brakes fixed soon. When I came home from work that night, exhausted and frustrated, wondering how I was going to afford to pay for that ticket, I discovered that our house had been broken into. My housemate Hillary had gotten home just before me and was sitting in one of the dining room chairs eating a late snack with her plate in her lap. I walked in and noticed that my stereo was missing, as well as most of my CDs.

"Uh, do you know if someone borrowed my stereo and CDs, Hillary?" I asked, hoping to hell that I hadn't just been robbed, once again. My previous record as a victim of theft was almost sadly, pathetically comical. My backpack had been stolen while I was in Europe, sleeping on a bridge in Paris. My car had been vandalized at a trailhead while I was camping with a friend just a few months before moving to Eugene; and my next car had been stolen six months later while I was visiting my aunt and uncle in Portland, only to be found a few weeks later pretty banged up. And as I mentioned before, my mountain bike had been stolen shortly after I moved to Eugene.

Unfortunately, as Hillary and I started to look around the house, we realized that it had indeed happened again. We never locked the back door for the simple reason that it didn't lock. Apparently someone had been aware of this, or else had gotten lucky trying random doors, and had come into the house sometime during the day while the four of us were out of the house. Almost everything I owned of value had been taken. In addition to my stereo and CD collection, the thief had ripped off my backpack, hiking boots, and Nikon camera.

Over the next few weeks, it hit me that I was definitely going to be leaving Eugene soon. I had no certain idea of where to go from there, but I couldn't easily deny the message of everything manifesting in my life lately: it was time to make a major shift of some kind.

The final and decisive reason I saw that it was time to leave was that the lease for our house was going to run out at the end of September, and my housemates had decided to look for another place together. Due to the $150 I owed for the traffic ticket, plus the fact that I hadn't put down a rental deposit when I'd initially moved into the house, I wasn't sure if I could afford to go in on another place with my housemates. And I didn't feel much like trying to find a cheaper room in another household with another group of new people to get to know.

What I most wanted at that point was just to sell everything I owned, including the pickup, pay off all my bills, hit the road, and hike far out into the desert somewhere, alone, with no distractions, no expectations, nothing to do but simply *be* for a while—and hopefully figure out, to some extent, what was really going on with all these events swirling around me. I decided to work through the end of September, to save up some money to keep me going for a while, then sell my truck and hit the road. Although it had been a while since I'd done any hitchhiking, I looked forward to it. I'd been driving around town for my two delivery jobs for the past year and welcomed the thought of just being a passenger going along for the ride.

After a four-day backpacking trip in the Oregon Cascades with my brother, at the end of that summer, he left Eugene himself to head back down to Santa Cruz for another year of school. He took along with him a few of my few boxes of unnecessary belongings to store in my mom's garage—while I was gone to wherever it was that I was going next. The appropriateness of leaving began to feel more and more certain, despite the profound unknown that lay ahead of me.

After the four of us moved out of our house at the end of September, I stayed for two weeks on the floor of my old housemates' new house, working and wrapping up final business as well as formulating a plan for where I would go once I left Eugene. My plan involved a number of mini-adventures within the larger adventure of making my way progressively east to visit "Amy back in Austin" (there's a country song with that very title). I had no clue as to what might happen from there.

I intended first to stay for a few days at a yoga retreat center in Northern California called Ananda Village, which was founded by the author of a book I'd read recently, *The Path*, by Swami Kriyananda. I also planned to visit Yosemite National Park, the Grand Canyon, and perhaps a few other National Parks. And I was determined to spend some time alone in the desert.

A few days before I was to leave Eugene, I came across Jeffrey in town. It had been a while since I'd seen him. I was glad to be able to connect before taking off on my trip. He was pleased to hear that I was leaping into such an adventure of my own volition—he had made a similar decision years before when he'd suddenly quit school, sold all of his belongings, and became homeless, simply to facilitate personal and spiritual growth through the challenges the lifestyle would inevitably bring. Although I certainly didn't plan on being without a home indefinitely, I was up to the challenge for a few months, or at least until another option came forth. Jeffrey recommended a book to me, *Right Use of Will*, and then, with a deep gaze and a hug, wished me well on my journey.

On my way home that day, I stopped by the local metaphysical bookstore to get the book that he had mentioned. It had a beautiful symbol on the cover and was subtitled *Healing and Evolving the Emotional Body*. It seemed like just my style.

Following my last day of work at the pizza parlor, my final task was completed when I sold my old Datsun pickup truck a few days later, the day before I planned to leave. The next morning, I got a ride with a friend, Allen, who was in the mood for a little day trip down to Ashland in southern Oregon. He dropped me off in the center of the small, quaint town.

I gave Allen a hug goodbye, then started hiking through town, my loaded pack strapped to my back as evening descended, looking around for somewhere safe to throw down my sleeping bag for the night.

CHAPTER 9

I slept that night at home plate on the baseball diamond of an elementary school. The next day was Sunday, so I figured I wouldn't be bothered. I felt so unencumbered as I awoke in the morning to the sun shining down overhead, warming me after the chilly night. I just lay there for a while soaking up the warm rays, reveling in my newfound freedom. I had finally managed to release myself for a time (albeit with a little help from unexpected circumstances) from the weight of a job, house, car, bills, and cumbersome possessions. I could now focus on my cluttered mind and soul for a while and then tackle societal responsibilities when I had a better idea of what I really wanted to be doing with my life.

I felt a great lightness as I stuffed my sleeping bag and clothes into my pack, pulled on my Levis and tennis shoes, and hefted my pack onto my back. The chilly morning air inspired me to get moving as the warming sun promised a clear day free of rain. This was how life should be lived! The future was unknown and wide open, a blank canvas ready to be streaked with color—raw material waiting to be molded into a unique work of art. Although I no doubt had a certain apprehension at the unknown ahead of me, there was also a great deal of opportunity and potential, and I was willing to take the positive and negative hand in hand and see what might come out of it.

My first destination was Ananda Village outside of Nevada City in the foothills of the Sierra Nevada. I figured it would take about two days to hitchhike there. I felt that my journey had really begun as I stepped out onto the freeway with my thumb held high.

My first ride, just outside of Ashland on Interstate-5, was surprisingly from a trucker. Generally truck drivers no longer pick up hitchhikers in order to avoid lawsuits if they should get into an accident. But apparently, so he explained, those who drive their own rigs are more willing to take a chance and will occasionally pick up hitchers to have some company while traveling down the lonely road.

He took me all the way down I-5 to the Highway 99 turn-off. From there I caught a ride from a local man in a pickup to Chico, and then another to Highway 20 at Yuba City. At Yuba City, I got stuck walking the long, noisy three or four miles across town and over the bridge to neighboring Marysville, since there was nowhere along the way to continue thumbing. By the time I arrived at the edge of town outside Marysville, the sun was already going down. I hiked into a nearby orchard and slept under the stars for the night.

I made it to Ananda the next day. My final ride was from an aging hippie in a Volkswagen bug. The passenger door didn't open, and the passenger seat as well as the entire back seat was piled high with assorted junk. I stuffed my backpack through the window into the back seat, crawled in through the window, and perched on the pile of junk in the front seat, my head crooked against the ceiling. He knew where Ananda Village was and went a little out of his way to drop me off at the entrance to the community.

Ananda Village is a commune of about three hundred folks, based on the teachings of Paramahansa Yogananda, a Hindu yogi who came over to America from India in the 1920s. The community was founded in 1969 by one of his direct disciples, Swami Kriyananda, whose autobiography I'd recently read. Being interested in both yoga and intentional communities, I was excited to check the place out. I had been in contact with them before coming, so they were expecting me. I planned to do work exchange there for a week or so before continuing on my way.

I spent ten sublimely eventless days there—just what I had hoped for—doing yoga, meditation, light work in the kitchen and garden, and going on quiet walks through the surrounding dry forest. I spent the nights camped in my tent in a grove of trees across the meadow from the retreat, where many deer gathered to graze.

I found myself in awe at being among so many spiritually focused people gathered together at the same place. The spiritual quest was something I had been traversing for the most part alone over the past few years, as I became increasingly focused on inner development. To be with a group of people, all with a similar focus was a great reassurance. And, to top it off, the vegetarian food they served there was delicious. It was all just what I needed at the time.

But, despite the gentle people, light work, yoga, meditation, and good food, after a week I began to feel restless. I was ready to get on with my adventure. The void of the great unknown lay ahead of me. And I was ready to leap right into it. I packed up my few belongings late one morning and was given a sweet send-off by some of the community members. They formed a small circle around me holding hands, and as I stood in the center, they sang their simple goodbye song:

"Go with love, may joyful blessings guide you safely on your way. May God's light expand within you, may we be one in that light some day..."

I hitchhiked south down winding Highway 49 to Yosemite National Park, spending one night in the woods along the highway. I arrived at the park late in the evening after getting my last ride from a park service employee, who dropped me off in front of Yosemite's hiker/biker campground, which was only three dollars a night per person.

I found a site and paid for the next five nights, since the attendant had warned me that it might fill up quickly for the coming weekend. Then I set up my tent, unpacked my backpack, changed from my dirty Levis into a warm pair of clean sweatpants, crawled into my sleeping bag, and crashed.

I awoke late the next morning, my mind feeling groggy and clouded. The events of the past few months were suddenly descending on me all at once, feeling like a whirlwind thrashing around in my mind.

Just a few weeks earlier I had been leading a normal, fairly stable life. Now I was sleeping in a tent—and that tent pretty much encompassed all of my immediate belongings and responsibilities. The feelings that this sudden change brought up in me were simultaneously of freedom, personal power and excitement, and that age-old fear of that which we always instinctively wish to avoid—the unknown.

If it had been completely up to my mind where I would be in that moment, I would have reasoned that the last position I wanted to be come late October was sleeping outdoors and hitchhiking across the country, homeless and unemployed, with no concrete plan for where I would spend the winter. If reason and common sense was what mattered most at the time, I could have kept my job, found another place in Eugene, and perhaps sold my truck to cut back on expenses. But at least I would have been somewhere warm and dry for the winter, where I had friends and things were familiar and I had some measure of security. I could have saved money over the winter and then left on my experimental adventure the following spring, leaving plenty of time to find another place to call home before the next winter.

Of course, this isn't what I did, for a number of reasons. Some were practical and some were intuitive—my gut was telling me that this was the thing to do. Although the mind generally prefers to plan the future out beforehand in order to avoid unpleasant circumstances, deep down I must have known that I needed this experience—a symbolic leaping into the darkness—to crack me wide open. There was no other way to do it. I couldn't know in advance what was going to happen, because what I needed to contact within myself was totally unknown territory. I was about to venture into a deep, dark and terrifying part of my own consciousness. And I needed to trust those gut feelings—rather than my mind—to let it happen and somehow guide me through it.

Of course, I didn't realize all this at the time, having no prior knowledge of Kundalini energy, let alone that it was on the verge of awakening within me. And yet, Kundalini awakening is what everything in my life, subtly yet resolutely, seemed to be building towards. Kundalini rising within us is part of the process of healing those deepest feelings of fear, pain, and despair, that we all hold within ourselves, buried away in the recesses of our mind. These unpleasant, to say the least, inner struggles have something important to teach us. But they need to be brought up and experienced before they can truly be healed.

There is really no way (at least in my admittedly subjective experience) to awaken the Kundalini without facing some level of fear, doubt, turmoil, confusion, desperation and plenty of other so-called "negative" emotions and psychic imbalances. Along with the Kundalini energy comes all of these deepest human feelings buried deep in our subconscious mind. The subconscious corresponds with the root chakra, the source of the Kundalini energy. Allowing these feelings to awaken, be experienced, validated, and brought back into the light of consciousness will help bring the deeper presence of love and healing to Earth, that is so necessary during this time of tremendous transition.

I spent five days exploring the picturesque Yosemite Valley. It felt like a vast, limitless playground. I hadn't been there since visiting with my family as a child. I relived some old memories as I hiked the many trails, crossed rushing rivers, and meditated near the bottom of splashing waterfalls. After the past few months of stress and confusion, it was just what I needed: to spend some real time in nature and attune to its vibration. Since it was October, Yosemite wasn't as crowded as usual, so there was actually some peace and quiet to be found there. And despite all the hype around Yosemite, it still has some of the most striking natural scenery in the world.

I had been planning on spending a few more days there, until the campground attendant informed me that there was a huge snowstorm headed towards us at that very moment, expected to arrive later that evening. It was mid-morning when I heard this news, and I didn't feel at all like hurriedly packing up my things, and then getting back out on the road, but neither did I want to spend the next three or four days freezing cold in my tent through a snowstorm. And if I was going to get out of there ahead of the storm, then I had to hurry.

An hour or so later, I was packed up and out on the road, with my thumb out and a cardboard sign that read, "Joshua Tree or Death Valley." The only problem was that apparently everyone else in the park (those with cars and thus radios) had been informed of the impending snowstorm well before I had. There was hardly any traffic leaving the park. I ended up standing there for hours, admiring Half Dome in the distance, and the beautiful fall colors all around me—but becoming increasingly anxious to get the heck out of there.

Finally I got a ride, but the driver was only going a few miles down the road, and he left me in a worse position than before, since now I couldn't walk back to the campground if I didn't get a ride before nightfall. I started looking around for possible places to set up my tent, in case I had to ride out the storm, which was starting to feel like a real probability, as the clouds started pouring in overhead, the temperature dropped, and it started getting dark.

Finally, as the last bit of evening light was beginning to fade, I got a ride from a German tourist named Hans in a VW van, who was headed all the way to Las Vegas to do some gambling. I was overtaken with gratitude as I climbed into the warm vehicle, thanking the universe for coming through for me when I really needed it. It's amazing how often it works out that way.

We spent all that evening driving over the Sierra Nevada via Tioga Pass, just ahead of the storm. We slept that night warm and dry outside the van on the desert floor of Death Valley. The next morning, we continued on towards Las Vegas, arriving mid-afternoon. He dropped me off near the outskirts of the city.

It took three rides just to get out of Las Vegas, the last of which was with an older man honest enough to tell me that I ought to take a shower sometime. I definitely wasn't opposed to the idea, since I was feeling pretty tired and sweaty from the past two days of driving. I changed my shirt, in hopes that that might help, and continued hitchhiking. The sun was starting to go down, but I decided to keep hitching until dark, since I wasn't in the best place to find somewhere to sleep for the night.

I ended up getting a ride with a neurotic, loud-mouthed and (so he said) reformed alcoholic, who kept yelling obscenities out the window at all the other drivers. Other than that he didn't have much to say. I stayed with him on through Kingman, Arizona, and then to the desolate turn-off for the Interstate heading south towards Phoenix where he dropped me off. I was planning to go straight across Arizona rather than south. Besides, it was getting late, and he wasn't the best company, even by hitchhiking standards.

It was past midnight when he left me alongside Interstate-40, and I was exhausted. A soft motel bed would have really hit the spot right then, but there wasn't one in sight, and I couldn't afford it anyway. The best spot that I could find to throw down my sleeping bag ended up being between a huge cactus and a barbed wire fence, right next to the freeway on-ramp. Not quite what I had in mind, but oh well. I tossed down my pack, unrolled my sleeping pad, pulled out my sleeping bag, and then crawled in and attempted to get some sleep. All night, trucks coming from Phoenix beamed their headlights directly on me as they made the turn from one freeway to the other and roared past. Needless to say, I didn't sleep terribly well.

I had been debating whether or not to see the Grand Canyon, having never been there before. I decided to go ahead and check it out, since I would be going pretty much right past it. Perhaps I would hike down into the canyon, spend a few days in contemplation by the Colorado River, and come up with a few answers to life's big questions while I was at it.

I eventually got a ride east down the Interstate, to the turn-off heading north towards the Grand Canyon. The chilling realization of oncoming winter overtook me as I piled out of the car with my pack, said "Thanks for the ride," and then watched the car continue on down the freeway. I could see my breath as I stood there in the silence and wondered if I had made the right choice to hop out at that point. Obviously, we had gained some elevation in the last hundred miles or so.

I immediately pulled out of my backpack all the cold-weather gear I had. My breath was pouring out of me like a smokestack. I was reminded of something my brother said once: "The nice thing about being able to see your breath, is that you know you're breathing." The comfort these words of wisdom brought me didn't last too long, as I realized that I didn't have much in the way of cold-weather gear. Considering that I was making my way towards Texas, I hadn't been thinking too much about encountering cold.

At least I did have some thin gloves, an extra shirt, a warm pull-over and a headband, all of which helped. After re-packing and walk-ing a short distance up the road to a better spot for cars to pull over, I sat down on my backpack and waited.

A half-hour later, about two cars had passed. I was freezing cold, and starting to wonder if I was completely bonkers for even setting out on this ridiculous adventure. I had no long-term plans, I had al-ready spent most of the money I'd saved before leaving, and winter was—at least in northern Arizona—already here. But it was a little too late to change my course at that point, since I didn't really have anywhere to go back to. I resolved to make the best of it and trust that I was somehow on the right path.

I started a ride-calling dance to help me get a ride out of there—hopping around my backpack, letting out yips and calls, raising my arms into the air and yelling into the silence, "Please, Great Spirit, bring me a ride! Please, Great Spirit, bring me a ride!" over and over. If nothing else, it helped warm me up.

Just as I was beginning to wonder if I should forget the Grand Can-yon altogether and catch a Greyhound bus straight to Austin where at least it would be warm, I was rescued by a couple of Deadheads, Eric and Deirdre, and their cat Ripple (after the Grateful Dead song), in a Ford Econoline van. I climbed in, shivering but thankful.

Eric and Deirdre were on a road trip back to the East Coast after a terrible couple of months living in San Diego, and were stopping by the Grand Canyon for just a few hours. They offered to take me as far east as I wanted to go with them. But I said that I would probably get out at the canyon, since I really wanted to hike down into it.

Once we got there, however, my plans quickly changed. It was snowing. As mentioned, I wasn't fully prepared for the cold. Although it would have been warmer at the bottom of the canyon, 5,000 feet below, it wasn't worth taking the risk. After hanging around on the edge of the canyon for a little while, ooohing and aaahing in wonderment, the three of us went into the tourist trap of a restaurant for coffee and French fries. Soon enough we were all piled into the van and back out on the road.

We drove all through that day and late into the night, through a huge snowstorm. We slept in the van for a while at a rest stop before continuing on the next morning. They dropped me off in the small town of Santa Rosa in eastern New Mexico. From there I planned to hitch down towards either White Sands National Monument or else Carlsbad Caverns.

I spent that morning doing laundry and checking out the town, which I soon discovered was predominantly Native American and Latino. Though I felt very respectful of Native American spirituality and culture and had worked with many Latinos for my dad's construction company, I began to notice that the vibe I was getting there wasn't particularly welcoming. I started to get a little worried about getting a ride out of town.

After waiting at the edge of town for only a few minutes, my fears were realized when a beat-up old station wagon full of young men squealed by. One of them stuck his head out the window just long enough to curse at me, "Fuck you and your ride, you stupid piece of shit!"

While standing there numbly for a little while trying to decide what I should do next and what the message was here (although it was pretty obvious, literally at least), I looked around me and realized that I was right on the edge of the desert that I had so wanted to spend time immersed in. With that, I strapped on my pack and buckled it tight, hiked a little farther down the road away from town and the Interstate, and then hiked into the desert.

I spent four days out in the desert, going once into town for water. In four long days I didn't do much of anything, really. I slept, ate, wrote in my journal, meditated, and listened to music on my walk-man. I had some marijuana with me (which I still smoked very oc-casionally, generally in natural settings—the desert was perfect), and got high a few times; then I hiked around the desert in the warm, but not overbearing sunshine. This experience, of getting high in the open expanse of the desert, reminded me of a solo road trip I'd taken the summer before, just prior to moving into the Pearl Hill House…

It was mid-August, a few days after my second car had been re-turned after being stolen in Portland, and I needed some time away from the city to relax and clear my mind. I'd left Eugene after dark, heading east on Highway 126. I spent that night in the back of my station wagon at Hippie Hollow, the free campground near Cougar hot springs. I woke up the next morning to frost on the windows and the sun rising into a clear sky. I started up the car, turned on the heater, ate a bowl of granola in the front seat, and soon was headed down the road. It didn't take long to leave behind the lush forests of western Oregon.

At Bend, two hours east of Eugene and at the edge of the Oregon desert, I turned south for an hour and then east once again, down a lonely, dusty road that, according to my map, went right by a large lake in the middle of the desert. I thought that it would make a nice place to camp for the night. I never found the lake, though—it must have been a seasonal lake, and a shallow one at that—and I ended up driving most of the day through the seemingly endless desert. Finally, tired of driving, I pulled over at a wide turn-out along the dirt road, and turned off the car.

The immediate silence made me a little self-conscious, as I sat there in the car waiting for the dust to settle. Months in the city had filled my mind with clutter. Now it was all being magnified. Instead of the comforting drone of distraction that the city offers, it was just me and the desert, face to face. And the desert has an uncanny ability to act as a mirror, reflecting the self. In this case, it was an anxious, yet expectant self I witnessed. I was there to take a good, hard look within, willing to face whatever I found—and then hopefully manage to transform it.

The sun was beginning to go down as I threw a tarp on the ground and rolled out my sleeping bag. I cooked a quick meal on my camping stove, crawled into my sleeping bag and lay on my back, watching the stars, staring into the darkness and thinking about infinity.

How could the universe go on forever? The very thought of forever was too immense to even attempt to comprehend. And yet, how could it just end? Neither possibility seemed like an acceptable option. There seemed to be no compromise between these two extremes, yet there was no other plausible answer to that fundamental scientific, and philosophical, question: Does the universe end somehow, somewhere? The only resolution seemed to be in accepting that I didn't know and could never truly grasp the nature of the universe within the confines of my rational mind.

Well, then, to hell with reason! If reason was what stood between myself and the mystery of the universe, then I would just have to let it be shattered by the stark truth of not-knowing and leap straight into the depths of infinity—my own awareness of being. For what was more mysterious than that? Perhaps the answer was easier to find within anyway. Even with the most powerful telescopes, we couldn't reach the edges of the universe. But with the heart or the soul, could I find a different sort of answer to that age-old question? Either way, I knew that was where I needed to focus my energies and look for discoveries. Peering out into the vastness of the stars was almost like peering into your own soul anyway. It sure as hell makes you think, question, and wonder.

I slept long and hard and awoke to the sun rising from the desert floor, drying the dew from my sleeping bag. I had another bowl of granola for breakfast and then packed up and continued down the dusty road.

That evening, I came across a free and almost empty campground, in the middle of eastern Oregon, with desert all around. I found a nice campsite, parked, started setting up camp, and collected some wood to make a fire later on. Then I hiked out into the desert as the evening light was beginning to fade.

I found a spot on a ledge overlooking sparsely vegetated rolling hills and sat down on the ground cross-legged with my eyes closed for a few minutes. The moon was almost full—in fact, it was to be a blue moon in a few days. There was almost complete silence, except for the wind rustling through the sagebrush. I pulled my pipe out of my shirt pocket, filled it with some pot, took two or three hits, and then sat there on the ledge with eyes open and did my best to open to the nothingness.

As I became more and more high, I felt my awareness begin to expand, and the presence of the desert—and thus myself—grow stronger and stronger, to the point of deep uneasiness. I started to get a little freaked out by the silence and emptiness around me. But I did my best just to sit there and feel it, to recognize my fear for what it was—trapped energy that merely needed to move through me and be released.

As I concentrated on feeling the fear and letting it go, waves of energy began flowing up my spine, one after another—engulfing me, and then flowing out the top of my head. It was fairly subtle, nothing like what I would experience later. But I was clearly releasing some inner energy of some sort, and in so doing I began to feel more relaxed, grounded, and attuned to the environment of the desert. My anxiety was transformed into peaceful presence and a feeling of spiritual fulfillment.

As the waves of energy slowed, I stood up and turned around. Seeing my moon-shadow on the ground below me had the peculiar effect of making me want to fly. I raised my arms up like wings, and closed my eyes, pretending that I was taking off from the ground—soaring high above the desert, over rolling hills bathed in the eerie black-and-white moonlight. I imagined the profound freedom that I would have felt as I looked down at everything so far below, the wind rushing by as I soared through the air. I could almost have believed that it was real.

I wasn't quite sure of my plans once I left the desert outside of Santa Rosa, New Mexico. The more I thought about Amy, the more I wanted to be with her. But other than a few postcards I'd sent along the way, I hadn't actually communicated in person with her in almost three months. I had no idea how she really felt about me now, or if there was anything left of the fragment of a relationship we had shared over the summer. I finally decided that the only way to find out for sure was to give her a call, before actually showing up on her doorstep.

I took down my tent from my desert camping spot and packed up the rest of my belongings late in the afternoon. After four days in the desert I felt strong, clear, and present. At the same time, I felt such intensity within my soul that it was almost too much to contain. I was getting so tired of wandering alone through the world, stumbling and bumbling along on this confusing, mystical spiritual quest. What was I really doing out here in the middle of the desert in late October? I yearned so deeply to know the real purpose of this path I walked—which more often seemed to be guiding me, rather than being guided *by* me.

I strapped on my backpack and hiked the two miles back to the highway and into the town of Santa Rosa, intending to stay that night in a cheap hotel. I found one for $20 and checked in, relieved to finally get to sleep on a soft bed, in an enclosed room for a change, with a shower, flush toilet and TV—those domestic comforts that I wished to remove myself from at times, but definitely still appreciated. I took a long, hot shower, then sat down on the bed and called Amy.

Her mom answered (she was staying with her mom while looking for her own place), and said she would get her. Finally, there was Amy's voice at the other end of the line.

"Amy?" I said.

"Yes?" she said softly.

"Hello, this is Gabriel…How are you?"

"Gabe! I'm all right…how are you? Where are you?"

"I'm in New Mexico. I just spent a couple of days in the desert. I'm pretty good. I'm not really sure what I'm doing out here, but here I am. Do you still want me to come visit?"

"Of course!" she said. "Actually, this is great timing. I just got an apartment on the other side of town, and I'm moving into it in a few days. So you should come after that, maybe in a week, so you don't have to stay here at my mom's. You can stay as long as you want."

"Great!" I said, feeling a wave of relief and some excitement at the prospect of finally seeing her again. "I'll hang out in New Mexico for a little while longer before coming down. I'm thinking of taking Greyhound, because the hitchhiking around here has been kind of lousy..."

We talked for a little while about things in general. It was so wonderful to hear her voice. And it was reassuring to find that she still wanted to spend some time with me; although, after saying goodbye and hanging up, I realized that I couldn't tell what sort of relationship she was interested in at this point—if, like myself, she was seeking a partnership, or if she only wanted to spend some time together as I was passing through. I figured that the only way to know was to go to Austin and see what might happen.

The next morning, as I was trying to figure out where to go hang out for a whole week, I noticed a town on the map that claimed to have some hot springs. Being a hot springs enthusiast, I decided to check it out. It was named "Truth or Consequences"—after a game show during the fifties, which had paid them a large sum of cash to change it from their previous name of, appropriately, Hot Springs, to that of the game show—and was located in southern New Mexico.

After my previous experience trying to hitch out of Santa Rosa, I didn't feel too comfortable giving it another try, so I decided to go Greyhound. I hopped on the bus that afternoon, backtracked west to Albuquerque, then south down to "T or C," as they called it, arriving late that night. I got another hotel room, despite my dwindling finances, not wanting to try and find a safe place to sleep out so late.

The next morning, after taking advantage of my money spent on the room by sleeping in, I checked out the phone book and discovered that there was a youth hostel right in town, with its own hot springs.

I walked out to the hostel at the edge of town, right along the Rio Grande (which wasn't looking very grand, but rather puny in mid-November) and paid for an affordable bed in their dormitory for the night. I spent the rest of the day sitting in the springs, reading, and writing in my journal on the deck overlooking the river.

I ended up spending five more relaxing days there, soaking in the springs, hanging out with the other travelers, writing in my journal, and doing plenty of contemplation—of both the past and the future. By the time I left the hostel, I felt ready to tackle whatever unknown lay before me. I had a sense that, whatever it was, it was likely to be pretty challenging. I was definitely right about that.

I caught another Greyhound from T or C to El Paso, Texas, and then from El Paso to San Antonio, staring out the window through the long 10-hour trip, mesmerized by the constant flow of people and places. I called Amy when we arrived in San Antonio. She said she would pick me up in an hour at the Greyhound station in Austin.

CHAPTER 10

My experience in Austin unfortunately was not—to say the least—the pleasant romantic interlude that I had anticipated. It was at first great to see Amy and Lisa, as I stepped off the bus to their smiling, familiar faces, and gave them big hugs, though I did notice that the connection between us wasn't quite the same as it had been during the wild adventures of the summer. After all, we'd only actually spent around a week together, in the course of our few brief visits.

After going out for Mexican food and then driving back to Amy's apartment, they were planning to go to a friend's party and invited me to come along. But it was already late in the evening, and I was feeling exhausted from the daylong bus ride, as well as overwhelmed by things in general—wondering in part of me what the heck I was even doing out there in the middle of Texas. And so I decided to stay behind at Amy's apartment, unpack my few belongings, and try to sort some things out. To complicate matters, later that night when Amy got home, she informed me, almost apologetically, that she was actually seeing someone else—and hoped it wouldn't bother me if he stayed over occasionally while I was visiting.

This was, in fact, rather devastating news, though I tried my best to hide how I felt. A wave of sadness and dashed expectations crashed over me, as my desire for a relationship was suddenly shattered. I had tried not to have too many expectations, knowing that things might not work out as I hoped—but they had been there nonetheless.

I felt a lot of adoration for Amy. Though she was a few years younger than myself, she had a strength and maturity amidst her beauty and femininity that was very attractive. I had truly enjoyed the time we'd spent together over the summer. Though we had never made love, we'd slept together a number of nights, kissing and caressing one another. We'd felt a mutual trust and intimacy, as best as I could tell at least, that let us open our souls to one another.

But all that we had previously shared felt suddenly like a past life, as I realized that, as part of me had feared, Amy had not had a similar desire to continue our relationship from where we'd left it months before. She had merely invited me to visit as one friend offering another friend a place to stay for a little while.

But why, then, had she said that I could stay as long as I wanted? Especially in a one-room studio, while she was seeing someone else? Her open-arms invitation over the phone certainly didn't convey the fact that she was already in a relationship with somebody. I couldn't piece it together. I found myself awash in disappointment, growing into frustration as I wondered what to do next with my life, where to go onwards from there.

But at least, amidst all the miscommunication, we were still glad to see one another, and tried to make the best of the situation. She seemed sincere about letting me stay as long as I wanted or needed. Since I didn't know where I was going next, I resolved to stay with her for a while and try to enjoy the time together. Maybe it would work out for the best. There must be some reason why I had come all the way out here, even if it wasn't readily apparent. Perhaps it would work out for me to live with her through the winter, save up a little money, and then have the spring and summer before me to make up my mind what I was doing next in my life.

However, after I'd met her boyfriend, Michael—a nice, somewhat eccentric 29-year-old musician—a few days later and noticed my feelings of resentment in response to their exchange of affection, it became clear that I wasn't going to end up enjoying myself much while I was there.

After a week, I decided that I needed to leave Austin as soon as I could. It was just too painful to stay there, wanting so badly to share love with the woman I had come all this way to see, unable to get close to her. The only way I could think to resolve the situation was simply to remove myself from it.

But I couldn't leave right away, since not only did I not know where I was going, I was also just about broke. I'd spent too much on the Greyhound ticket and motel rooms, and was now down to barely enough cash to last another week or two. I concluded that I'd better find a job and make a little money. In the meantime, I could make up my mind about what to do next.

I soon found a job, at a deli not far from Amy's apartment, and started working 30 hours a week. Though I disliked it, I knew that I wouldn't be there long. I had a number of options forming as to where to go from Austin. I thought I might go back to Ananda and do work exchange there through the winter; go up to Alaska and visit my best friend from college, and maybe stay there for a little while; or go live with my mom in Northern California and take a few classes at the local community college. I also sent an application to a state university in Northern California for the next fall.

Though Amy and I lived together in the same little apartment for over a month, sadly, we spent only occasional time together and didn't get much closer than we had been over the summer. If anything, we closed ourselves more than we opened. Either I was busy working, or downtown hanging out at the library and bookstores; or she was gone working herself, or spending time with Michael. And when we were together, we didn't really know what to say about the difficult situation, other than to try to get along in spite of it. It was typical miscommunication, proving particularly painful for me, since she was the only friend I had in the area.

Over that month I went into a downward spiral of loneliness. In addition to the challenging living circumstances, I was on my usual spiritual roller coaster—except that I didn't have anywhere to really deal with things, and thus couldn't resolve or heal everything that was surfacing within me. Having no outlet, my unexpressed thoughts and emotions began backing up in my consciousness, so that I felt as if I were carrying around a heavy weight. I wasn't sleeping well, and I felt groggy and cloudy much of the time.

I was smoking hand-rolled cigarettes a few times a day, which I smoked on occasion while traveling—but which wasn't helping my emotional state much, or my health. One night, after staying late in a local bookstore and then sitting on a bench for a while in front of the University of Texas, smoking and watching the people walk by, I suddenly felt as if my heart were skipping beats. It scared me to hell, to say the least, especially when the irregularity didn't cease. I even feared that my heart might stop. And then, for a moment, I thought that it actually had stopped, until I felt it start up again.

I held my hand over my heart to confirm that it was still beating regularly, as I tried to make sense of what was going on here, before I totally freaked out. I put out my cigarette as my heart continued its irregular palpitating, and did my best to monitor the situation. I couldn't tell quite what the problem was—whether it was actually my body going haywire, or just my mind. All I knew for certain was that something frightening was going on, and that it was scaring the shit out of me.

I finally concluded that I had better check into a hospital, since I didn't want to risk dying of a heart attack right then, if that might possibly be what was happening. After looking in the phone book to find the closest one, I walked towards the hospital, my hand clutching my heart, trying not to lose myself in fear and desperation. Once I found the hospital, I went to the emergency room, stood in line, and then explained my problem to the nurse at the counter.

"Well, there could be any number of explanations for your symptoms. We can give you some tests that might tell us what's going on, if you really think it's that serious," she said.

"Are they expensive?" I asked.

"Well, a couple hundred dollars for each one, here in the emergency room. There are four or five different tests, that may or may not identify the problem."

"Wow—yes, that is a little expensive," I said, as I thought to my-self, "a thousand bucks to *maybe* find out what's wrong? I can't be-lieve this is happening!" Tears were beginning to form, as I pondered my aggravating dilemma. Why in the world was I creating this real-ity? What was the lesson here? What was it all leading up to?

"Well, I'll have to think about it," I told the nurse. Of course, I didn't want to take a risk with my life—but neither did I want to run up a bunch of bills if it wasn't absolutely necessary. I decided instead to trust in the universe, and hope that I wouldn't die inexplicably that night of heart failure. I walked out of the hospital and made my way through the darkened city streets towards Amy's apartment, praying that I would be all right.

Amy was gone when I arrived. My heart seemed to have calmed down a little during my walk, though my mind was still running wild. Everything I'd experienced the last few weeks and months seemed to be flooding my consciousness, threatening to overwhelm me with sensory overload on all levels. I wanted to yell out loud in frustration, cry in anguish, moan, wail, and grieve. I wanted someone there to talk to about everything, someone to help me sort out this bewilder-ing experience. But instead I felt a gaping darkness opening up all around and within me that seemed beyond explanation or reason.

Would I ever find the peace that I desired? Was this all there was to my life, after years of digging within, expecting to find a jewel of real value? Where was the happiness that I had been trying to create all this time? What could I do from here that would somehow be an im-provement in my life? Had all the searching I'd done up to this point been completely useless? If so, then what was the point in living?

But I knew that death wasn't really an option. My desire to live and enjoy life was much too strong. As difficult as things might be at times, I was still thankful for all I'd experienced in my twenty-two years, and I knew that I had plenty to live for. I desperately wanted to find inner peace and happiness and be able to move on with my life. And I realized then that I had to leap right into the depths of everything that I was feeling, rather than try to escape it. I had to surrender to my experience if I really wanted to change it. I had to face the darkness, journey to the heart of the unknown, and discover what was really waiting for me there. I stripped down, crawled into my sleeping bag on the floor, lay down on my back, and closed my eyes in meditation, feeling somehow as if I were falling into a deep, dark abyss within my soul.

PART 3

Climbing the Canyon

CHAPTER 11

The months following my unexpected Kundalini awakening were a hell that can hardly be conveyed. Although the first few days were the most severe, the intensity and duration of what followed was beyond anything I could have previously imagined. The closest approximation is a nightmare drug trip that never ends. I found myself in the depths of true spiritual and psychological anguish. I felt as if my soul were being slowly, mercilessly tortured in a downward journey that could only end in something bordering on madness. The next few months were a test of will that took all of my strength, and even more than I knew I possessed, to endure.

After coming home abruptly from Texas to spend Christmas with my dad and brother in the Bay Area, I moved in with my mom and step-dad at their house in Ukiah, in Northern California, near where I'd grown up. I enrolled in a math class at the local community college, which I needed to complete before transferring up to Humboldt State University the next fall; and then got a job working at the college library. Taking that one class and working fifteen hours a week at the library was all I could handle amidst the onslaught of conflicting psychic energies that were constantly engulfing my body, mind, and soul. I found myself engaged in an ongoing desperate struggle for survival that seemed, at the time, to have no conceivable resolution.

Over the first two months after moving in with my mom, almost every night I lay down on my bed feeling certain that I wouldn't live to see morning. The burning at the base of my spine and lower back was so profoundly, acutely painful, that I was convinced that even if I were to survive it, I would somehow end up maimed or paralyzed in the process. Whether or not this made any rational sense didn't matter much; somehow it seemed like a real possibility at the time.

Day after day I was hit by random waves of electric shocks throughout my body and consciousness that left me shaken, battered, disoriented, and paranoid. The electric current rushing through my body—especially at the tops of my hands and feet—felt at times as if it might actually fry my flesh. My bones took on the feeling of hard, cold, electrified metal. My muscle control seemed to be impaired so that eating, walking, and hand-eye coordination required great attention and concentration, due to an apparent gap of some sort between my mind's command and my body's response.

My nervous system, as a whole, had gone completely haywire. I would regularly wake up in the middle of the night in agony, overwhelmed by flashes of light within my mind and appearing visibly all around me, that were so intense I feared they might render me blind.

Energy was manifesting through me in so many different forms, I could hardly keep track of what I was experiencing. I felt simultaneously as if I were being crushed, pummeled, and constricted into nothingness; as well as being pulled apart in all directions, on the verge of being ripped into shreds. I was continually being pushed, pulled, bombarded, hit, twisted, and squeezed by the tremendous force rising spontaneously within me. And on occasion I could feel a subtle, yet powerful pulsation coming from somewhere in the vicinity of my root chakra, like the roar of a great machine, surfacing momentarily to reveal the source of my anguish.

I went on many long walks to distract myself. Though nothing seemed to truly alleviate my turmoil, at least walking in the woods at the edge of town served as a diversion and helped a little to channel the extraordinary flood of energy rushing through my mind and body. Given that I didn't know what else to do, I just had to stay with it as best I could and hope that things would improve over time.

But I should mention that ultimately, in my experience at least, the only way to truly align with this force is to bring it directly through your being—allowing it rise to up through all of the chakras and puri-fy them. Denying it, ignoring it, or finding other channels for the en-ergy that move it out or away from you will only prolong the time it takes to transform the nervous system. Once the Kundalini has been activated within an individual, there seems to be no way to shove it back down or to get around dealing with it. It has to be allowed to come into the chakric system, flow freely and work its magic—or it will simply remain in a state of imbalance and ungroundedness, and thus continue to be experienced as pain, rather than as the deep vi-tality that is its true nature. Once the Kundalini power is fully awak-ened, it cannot effectively be controlled or overpowered, it cannot be avoided, it cannot be accepted within constricting limitations of the mind, it cannot be channeled around the self, because the pain of its coming into one's soul is too much to bear. Once arisen, Kundalini will take you on a wild ride that won't let up until it has found total acceptance and balance.

Again, this is purely my own experience and subjective under-standing. Not all who undergo Kundalini awakening go through the same challenges that I faced. The experience is particular to each in-dividual—some apparently report simply experiencing a rush of bliss that invigorates their mind; others say that they find themselves un-able to sleep, yet fully energized, for weeks at a time; others have something resembling an out-of-body experience. There are plenty of books on the subject (which I eventually came across, months after my experience).

Pain and suffering relating to Kundalini is, as always, simply a matter of imbalance and blocked energy of some sort. If the chakric centers are fairly open and clear when the Kundalini is activated, less pain will be experienced, because there are fewer blockages in the energy's path as it rises to the crown chakra. I guess that I had my share of roadblocks in the way that needed to be rammed through. I know that's more or less what it felt like.

Ultimately, Kundalini is simply the pure energy of conscious be-ing. It has the power to fully clear our physical, mental, emotional and spiritual bodies, if we allow it to. It is a positive force, even if it can be difficult to deal with in many cases. But be careful—awakening the Kundalini by trying to force it can be dangerous, as the power of this energy might be beyond a person's ability to handle. Heart attacks may, in some circumstances, actually be the result of premature Kundalini arousal. The heart center is the balancing point between the crown chakra and the root chakra. If the mind is overwhelmed by this force and can't stay present enough to balance with it, the heart may simply give up and quit. I don't think it's a coincidence that I was having heart trouble myself, just prior to my Kundalini awakening.

The electric shocks that I was experiencing, I realize now, were the result of my mind coming into contact with the lower-chakra Kundalini fire and struggling to integrate with it. If viewed in terms of electro-magnetism, then the mind, or thought, is the positive, electric force (masculine), and the Kundalini is the negative, magnetic force (feminine). Whenever they touched one another, I experienced a sudden electric shock, as the magnetic and electric forces snapped back together. These two apparently opposing energies were actually trying to find balance and alignment within my consciousness—though it felt more like a battle raging through me.

Seen in a broader context, these two energies of masculine and feminine have been battling one another all through human history, as men and women struggling to find balance with each other— women generally being subdued, suppressed and oppressed by men. Putting the pieces together, I can now understand one of the reasons why men can be afraid of women's power—when experienced out of balance, it feels like an electric shock!

But one must understand that these imbalances, in the form of electric shocks and everything else that was occurring within my nervous system, do not have to last indefinitely. This is merely what one may feel as these polarized energies come back together into their more natural state of union, and the old charge of tension is released. It may feel more like a terrifying collision than union at the time, since there is so much contentious energy between the masculine and the feminine. But this is part of the process involved in healing their differences, so that they may experience one another as two aspects of a unified entity, rather than as two opposing forces.

In dealing with overwhelming Kundalini awakening, it is imperative to feel and listen to the energy as best you can. Allow it to tell you what it needs and inform you when you are correctly opening your consciousness to it. I found that it is important not to impose any regulated routines on the process, unless they really seem to be in sync with your own particular situation. The Kundalini energy must be allowed to evolve and develop as it needs, and this may be drastically different in every moment. The symptoms and experiences from person to person seem to differ profoundly, and the different forms of healing needed for each individual will be equally varied.

Meditation isn't necessarily advised following the awakening of Kundalini (according to a number of sources I came across), because of the tendency for the mind to try to control the energy, either by increasing the flow to force it through, or else by suppressing it. Either tactic will serve only to heighten the pain experienced. Ultimately, of course, it is different for everyone, and so the real test is merely to try whatever you think might help and see how it feels. It will be fairly obvious what is or isn't effective in the healing process. If your approach is denying the Kundalini energy, it will create greater pain, whereas if it allows the energy to flow freely through your chakric system, then you should feel more relaxed, centered, and grounded.

In regards to diet, I would recommend trying different foods to discover what may or may not meet your individual needs. For example, if you're a vegetarian, you might consider eating meat. Although I was a strict vegetarian at the time, I wish that I had considered eating meat to see if it might have helped in the grounding process. Grounding is vital in handling the Kundalini energy. It can be achieved in many ways, one of which is through diet. Meat is a dense energy and may help to bring a person more into their body and lower-chakra energies and thus to anchor the energy. Basically, anything that helps you get your feet more firmly planted on the ground is probably a good thing.

And don't forget one of the most ancient and commonly practiced spiritual exercises—when in doubt, breathe! Too often, I've found myself in a state of stress and tension, only to realize that I'm not adequately breathing. Breath is indeed life, and deep breathing signals an intention and willingness to be in the present moment. No matter where you are or what you're doing, taking deeper breaths will likely be of great help, especially in the case of transmuting spiritual energies. Kundalini, prana and chi are all closely intertwined, and they may even be precisely the same thing, just different words. (I don't claim to be an expert on any of them, so someone else might disagree.) Either way, breathing deeply helps get the prana flowing; this in turn helps clear chakric blockages, where the energy needs to flow freely. The more you can help the Kundalini to carry out its intrinsic objective of unifying with the crown chakra, the quicker it will be able to evolve and transform your nervous system, and in so doing take you from a state of pain and desperation, to the spiritual healing and wholeness which is its ultimate goal.

Though it would be ideal to find guidance, suggestions, and healing techniques from an outside teacher who is experienced with this phenomenon, understand that, ultimately, *Kundalini itself is the teacher*. It might be more convenient if there were a simple, straightforward program to follow in dealing with these intense and erratic Kundalini symptoms. But in my understanding, this is not possible. Although you may have to go through it alone, there is much that can be done to ease the discomfort and facilitate healing while aligning with the energy. As mentioned, a key aspect of the healing process is to do whatever brings you more into your body. The experience of the electric and magnetic energies battling it out can be so painful that the reaction is to try to get out of what may seem to be the cause of the pain—the body itself. But the body only gives pain in response to energetic imbalance, and so is actually the most effective place to be if you want to heal—because it will tell you right where these imbalances are. If you go deeper into the pain and discomfort instead of moving away from it, then you can find its source and resolve it. Using the body in mutual cooperation with the more subtle spiritual energies is essential in facilitating healing.

If you don't know what to do, then try whatever you feel might help. Pay attention to the effects of whatever you try. Allow your deeper knowing/higher self to guide you through the process. Fully live the experience, to the extent that you can. Go walking or jogging, work in the garden, take lots of warm showers, go to hot springs, do yoga or tai chi, sing and dance, walk barefoot, meditate if you find it helpful, practice whatever spiritual discipline you normally practice, read about other people's experience with Kundalini (such as you're currently doing), and seek out people having similarly strange or difficult experiences. Basically, make a point of doing something, of getting out and living your life, rather than simply freezing up in fear and pain. It's remarkable how small, subtle things can completely change your point of view sometimes, just by getting the energy moving in the right direction. Basically, what it all comes down to is: Energy not moving is painful; energy moving feels good. So, do whatever helps you to get the energy moving.

In my case, to my extreme distress, I followed a route that led me through more pain and anguish before I began to experience anything that felt like real healing. To compound what was already unmanageable, unbearable pain throughout my physical, mental, emotional, and spiritual bodies, my suffering become greatly increased when I had an accident a few months after my initial Kundalini experience.

I was visiting my best friend from childhood, Abram, who was living in Willits (the town near where I was raised), about twenty miles north of Ukiah. He lived in a cabin on some land in the woods a few miles out of town, where he wrote, played music, and engaged in his many creative projects, when he wasn't working at the burrito shop in town, that he owned with his older brother.

One of his many creative projects was a skateboard ramp, which he had built along with his brother. I went to visit him one weekend and spent the night with him out at his cabin. In the morning, he took me out to show me the ramp. Having no skateboards with us at the time, we were just messing around on it in our bare feet, running up and down, back and forth on the slopes of the structure.

The north-facing slope was still wet with dew. Once, I jumped from the top of the ramp and, as I landed, my heal hit the dampened wood at such an angle that my foot slipped out from under me. I was thrown into the air almost upside-down and slammed back down onto the ramp on my neck and upper back. My entire back was suddenly engulfed in searing, excruciating pain, which stayed with me for months.

I didn't bother going to a doctor until a couple of months later, when I was able to get health insurance. I got X-rays and found that I was still healing from two hairline fractures to my vertebrae, one in the upper and one in the lower back.

Prior to this injury, which occurred mid-March, I was just beginning to see some light at the end of the dark tunnel that I had been trapped in for the past three months. But the injury crushed out the crack of light that had seemed to be appearing, and I was thrust back into suffocating darkness. I found myself in profound pain nearly every waking minute, and now even during my erratic sleep. What little sleep I did manage to find no longer gave me even the temporary relief of unconsciousness, leaving me little hope that there might be an eventual course out of my plight.

Upon my mom's suggestion, I began seeing a therapist. But having no knowledge of Kundalini and its effects, she was unable to really help me. Although it was comforting to have someone with whom I could share the pain of my experiences, simply talking about it didn't serve to truly alleviate the source of my symptoms. In fact, nothing I tried helped me much at that point. I was simply waiting in torment for something to somehow change.

At my therapist's suggestion, I started taking anti-depressants, since her assessment was that I must be experiencing physiological depression. I gave them a try, since I was open to anything. However, they did nothing but agitate my nervous system even more; and after a few weeks, I stopped taking them.

Later, I found a Buddhist teacher nearby, whom I began visiting regularly. And although his suggestions also were of some help, they didn't manage to fundamentally change the difficulty of what I was going through. The Kundalini energy was such that only a completely restructured nervous system could alter my response to its presence. And allowing this process to take place was, in my case, an intolerably lengthy and agonizing affair.

At one point, I came to the conclusion that, despite how deeply I desired to live, I had no way out but to kill myself. I felt that it was no longer possible to stay present with the pain that was with me every minute of every day. I had come to my breaking point again and again and had managed to go beyond it. But now I felt that I'd come across not just another hurdle, but rather the edge of a gaping crevasse that offered only the option of jumping headlong into the void. As far as I could tell, there was nowhere else left to go.

I thought about this possibility over a number of weeks. Slowly, I came to the conclusion that there were no other options available to me. I had tried everything I could conceive of. I'd endured for five months what felt like an eternity of hardship. I'd read countless books and sought out many teachers. I'd cried to God for answers and understanding. I'd waited and waited and waited for my condition to evolve. And yet I was still overwhelmed with these bizarre, terrifying symptoms of pain and torment that seemed to come from nowhere and yet were everywhere.

What else could I do but leave it all behind? From my perspective at the time, the situation seemed completely pointless. How could this be a necessary, meaningful experience in a loving universe—to be locked in unending, excruciating psychological and physical torture? What sort of God would allow such an experience? Why be a part of a world that permitted such seemingly senseless, ongoing suffering? I concluded that I would rather cease to exist than be trapped in this intolerable experience. There had to be a better place than where I was, in this life and this body.

At least I didn't plan to take my life right away. I'd read an article in *Outside* magazine, following the last summer I worked in Denali National Park. (I'd worked there summers while attending the University of Alaska.) This article told about a young man, Chris Mc-Candless, who had starved to death just outside the park during the same summer that I was there. After leaving his home on the East Coast and hitchhiking across the country, he had made his way up to interior Alaska, hiked alone into the snow-covered tundra just north of the park boundary, and tried to live off the land. He came across an abandoned school bus—an emergency shelter for hunters during winter—and lived in it through the late spring and into the summer, while he hunted and foraged for food.

He realized eventually that there wasn't enough food out there to keep him well fed and, besides, he was ready to get back to civilization. But what he didn't know was that he had crossed a frozen river along the way. When he tried to hike back out to the highway, he found that the rushing river, which had thawed in the previous months, now trapped him. He didn't know that he could have simply followed the river down to the busy Denali Park road, crammed with tourist buses. Instead, he hiked back to the abandoned bus and, over the next two months, starved to death.

McCandless had kept a journal, which was found along with his body at the end of the summer. In it he had chronicled his slow death by starvation. Although it had, of course, been painful, he recounted many moments of joy, and in the final few weeks of his life the pain and hunger were apparently replaced by an indescribable bliss. He seemed clearly to have experienced that which they call becoming "one with nature."

I decided that this was how I wanted to die. If I was going to leave this beloved planet behind, then I wanted do so in a state of peace and joy, even if it meant first enduring more pain in the process. I planned the coming summer around this decision to hike out into the wilderness and perhaps never return. After going to the annual Rainbow Gathering—in New Mexico that summer—I would fly up to Alaska. If at that time I still wished to die, I would hike into the tundra alone and there merge with the Divine. The silent, sweeping valleys and rugged mountains of Denali National Park, blanketed in tundra and willow bushes, populated with wild caribou, moose, mountain goats and grizzly bear, were the most inspiring surroundings that I could imagine for leaving this world.

CHAPTER 12

I shaved my head shortly before my twenty-third birthday, to signify the transition I would soon be going through—either that of miraculous healing in life, or else the awesome passage of death. Which path I might follow was still unknown to me. I knew only that it would be a profound challenge either way.

I finished up my library job and math class at the community college at the end of May. A few days later, with loaded pack on my back, I said goodbye to my mom and step-dad and left Ukiah for a summer that I knew would be filled with adventure and, hopefully, with peace and healing. I did in fact seem to be doing a little better than a few months earlier; my back was slowly mending, and the intensity of my symptoms had lessened slightly.

I hitchhiked twenty miles north from Ukiah up to Willits to visit Abram for a night before continuing northward. I intended to make my way up to Eugene to visit my friend Matt and my old yoga class and then head out to a small Oregon regional Rainbow Gathering in early June before going to the larger national gathering in New Mexico.

I ended up staying awake all night with Abram in his cabin, bullshitting, listening to music and playing basketball by the light of the half moon. The next morning, exhausted, I said goodbye, left Willits, and continued hitching north. Later that afternoon, I was somewhere north of Arcata, when I found myself too tired to continue on, due to lack of sleep the previous night. I was literally falling in and out of sleep as I sat on the side of the road with my thumb out. I decided to call it quits for the day, since I was in no big hurry. I hiked into a nearby field, lay my sleeping bag out in the tall grass, crawled in, and fell into a long, deep sleep.

For a change, I experienced the deep satisfaction that could come from good sleep. I had been sleeping so miserably the past few months, due to my injured back and Kundalini symptoms, that I hadn't been able to truly relax. But relaxation, of course, is essential for getting good sleep; and, as I've discovered, it's also important for allowing the Kundalini to flow through. I realized the importance of this as I awoke the next morning, after fourteen hours of deep sleep, feeling the most centered, calm and clear that I'd been in a long time. As the day progressed, however, many of my symptoms eventually returned, though I did continue to notice the improvement in my condition. Sleep deprivation had actually exhausted me to the point of relaxation, enabling me to fall into beneficial sleep.

I arrived in Eugene late that evening. I called my old friend Matt and stayed with him for the next couple of days. On my last night in Eugene, Matt, Sharon, and I drove out to McCredie hot springs, one of several in the area, out a different highway from the more well-known Cougar hot springs. After a long, hot soak together and some good conversation, Matt and Sharon headed back to Eugene, leaving me there alone. From there, I would head out to the Rainbow Gathering in central Oregon.

I camped that night in the woods near the steaming springs. After another soak the next morning, I packed up and hitched east over the Cascade Range, through the desert, and into one of the many National Forests of central Oregon. After standing for hours on a small gravel road in the middle of nowhere, I finally got a ride late in the afternoon from an elder hippie brother who was also headed to the gathering. We arrived later that night.

This small regional gathering turned out to be one of the most enjoyable Rainbow Gatherings I had been to. I experienced a closeness and belonging that I needed after the last six months of inner torment and loneliness.

It was a beautiful site amidst a thin, dry forest typical of eastern Oregon. Across a wide creek flowing through the trees was an open, delicate meadow—much of it roped off to prevent use—where we had our evening dinner circles. During my time there, I helped to cook and serve in the kitchen; built a plank bridge across the creek; hauled wood for the drum-circle bonfires; and helped build a sweat lodge. I also participated in the drum circles and the sweat lodge ceremony.

I'd been hoping I might see Jeffrey there. Midway through the gathering, I noticed him amidst a group of people near the main kitchen one afternoon, having just arrived. He looked very different from when I'd last seen him. He also had short hair—though not quite as short as mine, which was barely an inch long now after shaving it—and his beard was trimmed. I walked up and gave him a big hug. He was happy to see me, as I was to see him.

"You've changed," he said, peering into my eyes.

"Yes," I said. "It's been a hell of a journey, to say the least."

"Hey, me too..."

Talking to him later that afternoon, I found that he'd had a challenging time over the winter as well. He shared with me his experience of—as he described—his consciousness turning in an instant from a sharp sword into a puddle. He had lost some of his memory and had spent much of the winter moving through deep fear and confusion, same as me. It felt good to discover I wasn't the only one having a hard time finding balance in my life, and to be able to talk about it with him. I found the relative similarity of our experiences remarkable, though not terribly surprising. I knew that we were connected in some subtle way, though I couldn't fully make sense of it.

Towards the end of the gathering, I started looking for a ride out to the big national Rainbow Gathering in New Mexico. Although I had planned to stay a few days after the Oregon gathering to help with clean-up of the site, on the last official day of the festival I found a ride to New Mexico with a friendly couple headed straight to the gathering—Dream and Marie—in a large van. Two other folks were coming along—a man in his thirties named Forest, and a young woman named Bethany. It seemed like a fun crew, so I decided to go ahead and hop on board.

That afternoon, a big circle formed in the meadow for people to say their goodbyes and to express their enjoyment of the gathering. It had clearly been a powerful experience for many. People began standing in the center of the circle to share their gratitude for such a profoundly loving gathering and to share their heart-songs of the present and for the future. Some sang, some simply spoke, some shared a joke or two, but they all helped to bring the gathering to a close on a very pleasant note.

Before leaving, I went around the circle to where Jeffrey was sitting on the opposite side, to say goodbye. I gave him a big hug and then sat down and listened to what a few more people had to say, not wanting to go but knowing that my ride was packing up and getting ready to hit the road.

Just as I was about to leave, he pulled a large green stone from his pocket and placed it in the palm of my hand. "Sad Eagle," he said, nodding with a kind of inner realization. "I've been giving people names lately, based on how they feel to me. You seem like Sad Eagle."

"Thanks," I said, smiling. "Hopefully next year I'll be Happy Eagle, or maybe Playful Otter."

"I guess we'll see."

I gave him another hug, saying that I would see him soon. Then I left the circle, grabbed my pack from a nearby tree, and walked down the path towards the parking area. Dream, Marie, Forest, and Bethany were all there at the Ford van, finishing up the packing, and were glad to see me arrive. Within a half-hour we were back out on the dusty road, headed towards the 1995 National Rainbow Gathering near Taos, New Mexico.

Since all of us were pretty broke, we spent that night—all five of us—crammed together on a double mattress at the back of the van. Bethany and I were next to one another and ended up cuddling a bit. But none of us slept all that well, squashed together in the back of the van as we were. We decided we had to come up with a better plan if we were going to get any sleep over the next three or four days of traveling together.

But our plans were abruptly altered the next day anyway when the van broke down near Highway 395, just south of Susanville, California.

Dream had decided that he wanted to take us on a little side route up into the Sierra Nevada range just to the west, along the California-Nevada border, before venturing across Nevada. As we left Highway 395 and drove up a steep grade, he shifted into low gear. There was a horrible wrenching and grinding noise, and the van quickly coasted to a stop on the steep hill. Though the engine was still running, none of the gears would engage. The transmission was toast.

We coasted back down the hill to the main highway where I called my dad, got his AAA number, and then called a local towing company. They took the five of us and the van back north 30 miles, where they dropped us all off at Susanville Transmission. The van was backed into the garage, and Dream and Marie went inside to take care of business and await news of the damage.

Bethany, Forest, and I sat outside for a few hours, watching the traffic cruise down Main Street, reading and making music. Eventually, Dream and Marie came out of the garage with long faces, to tell us that the van needed a new transmission, and that it would cost about five hundred dollars to fix it—the same amount they had paid for the van a few months earlier. They didn't have enough to cover the cost, but didn't know what else to do. The mechanic had offered to buy the van for two hundred dollars, but they needed a vehicle, because all their personal possessions were with them—including a cat and a puppy. They couldn't possibly hitchhike all the way to New Mexico with everything they owned.

But they soon realized that they had little other choice. If they couldn't afford to fix the van, then they would have to sell it. They decided to accept the mechanic's offer of two hundred dollars, give away everything that wouldn't fit into their backpacks, and then hitch to the gathering with the cat and puppy.

They suggested that Bethany, Forest, and I should continue on the next morning. They would follow behind once they had organized their vanload of possessions. It was better to hitch in smaller groups anyway. The five of us spent that night sleeping scattered throughout the van, this time in the mechanic's parking lot. The next morning Forest, Bethany, and I said goodbye to Dream and Marie and that we would see them soon in New Mexico.

We hitched south to Reno, then east on Interstate-80 to the turn-off for Highway 50—the aptly-named "Loneliest Highway in America"—which headed straight into the desolate Nevada desert. From the junction at I-80, we got a ride down Highway 50 to the next small town, and then another ride about twenty miles into the desert. At that point we were dropped off in the absolute middle of nowhere.

We understood clearly then why this highway had its name. After an hour or so, only a few cars had passed. Considering our odds, we might be stuck there for days. It was the middle of the Nevada desert, it was summer, and there was no shade. After another hour and a few more cars—all of us fearing what felt like impending heatstroke—we built a makeshift shade-tent with some sticks lying around and a large shawl of Bethany's.

Another hour later, while Forest and Bethany sat under the tent waiting for a ride, I decided to stand on the other side of the road, and wait for cars heading back towards Reno. Given the situation, we decided that any ride that would get us the hell out of there was a ride we would take. We could then travel south from Reno, go through Las Vegas to Interstate-40, and then east through Arizona to New Mexico on a more well-traveled route.

Fortunately, we didn't have to. Forest came up with the idea of praying for a ride. "If we are very clear about what we want, and we ask for it with humility and intention, then we will get it," he declared. "So—what exactly do we want in a ride?" It was worth a shot—we had little else to do anyway.

We sat huddled under the shade-tent, as Forest wrote down on a small piece of paper: "Great Spirit, we ask for a ride from a kind, gentle, friendly and generous person, within an hour, who is going at least 500 miles."

We folded up the note and, along with some sagebrush that we had previously picked and dried, lit it on fire in one of my metal camping bowls. We sat in silence, holding hands in a small circle with our eyes closed as the paper and sage burned to ashes. When it had burned away completely, we emptied it into the wind with a simple "Amen."

"Well, that should do it," said Forest. "Now—we wait."

Half an hour later, our prayer was answered. A Subaru station wagon came flying down the road towards us. We all stuck out our thumbs enthusiastically. It passed us at first—then slowed down, turned around and came back. A young man got out.

"Hey, you guys! I almost didn't stop because my car is already pretty packed with my stuff. But we'll see what we can do."

His name was Drew, and he was a college student from U.C. Santa Barbara, heading back to his home in Denver for the summer. After twenty minutes of rearranging—tying much of his stuff onto the top of the car—he made just enough room for the three of us and our backpacks. We all climbed in, grateful to be moving and to feel that Great Spirit was indeed listening and looking out for us.

We stayed with Drew for the next two-and-a-half days, through the beautiful, lonely deserts of eastern Nevada, Utah, and western Colorado. By the time he dropped us off in the Rocky Mountains a thousand miles later, we were like old friends. We all hugged good-bye and wished each other well.

We were now practically within spitting distance of the Rainbow Gathering in New Mexico. And with some luck, we actually managed to make it there that evening, after getting a ride south to Durango, and then another from a farmer in a big pickup truck, who was headed for Taos. We all piled into the back. Bethany and I cuddled up together against the cab to keep out of the wind, and eventually fell asleep for much of the ride.

When, hours later, we came to the turn-off to the gathering a few miles before Taos—up a dirt Forest Service road marked with rainbow-colored ribbon—the farmer decided to give us a ride all the way out to the gathering. Though we warned him it might be a long haul up the dirt road, he assured us that it was no problem: he'd decided that, judging by the likes of us, he wanted to check out this unusual event for himself.

CHAPTER 13

Although the Rainbow Gathering in New Mexico was also an amazing experience, I went through a wide range of turbulent states during my three weeks there. My Kundalini symptoms were far from resolved. I was slowly learning to integrate what I was experiencing internally with my outer, daily life, but it was still a huge struggle. Every day I grappled with how to handle the intense energy flowing through my being without being totally overwhelmed by it.

Though the daily excitement of traveling proved in some ways more tolerable than the past six months at my mom's house in Ukiah, it was still difficult to find lasting balance with my symptoms, due in part to the new challenges that went along with the traveling lifestyle. My diet was erratic, my sleeping patterns were subject to whenever and wherever I might find somewhere to crash for the night, and my relationships with people were constantly shifting.

Though I had definitely improved since my despair of the spring, I was still immersed in a great deal of ongoing anguish, the end of which I still could not really envision. But at least it seemed that my condition was, in fact, improving over time, if slowly. All I could do was remain present with things as best I could, stay anchored in my body and mind, and hope that this was, eventually, guiding me to a state of healing and normalcy.

I came across Jeffrey once again a few days after arriving at the New Mexico gathering. He'd also had an interesting adventure getting there from the Oregon regional gathering. He had come with four other guys in another crazy van journey. They'd run out of money somewhere in Colorado and ended up busking (playing music on the streets) in Boulder for a few days before they (literally) drummed up enough gas money to get to the gathering.

Jeffrey mentioned that he was helping to set up a kitchen called "Om Chapati" and invited me to come help out. Over the next two weeks, I spent much of my time involved in the social goings-on there; glad to get some real time to hang out with Jeffrey and with the other kind folks while making hundreds of chapatis (an East Indian flat bread) as well as various dishes for the collective dinner at main circle.

Bethany didn't have her own tent and so ended up staying in mine for a while, since (to my surprise) it stormed almost daily throughout the gathering, often at dinnertime. Before arriving, I'd envisioned that it would be in the desert somewhere, since that was all I'd previously known of New Mexico. But northern New Mexico is actually much like western Colorado, being part of the Rocky Mountains. This gathering was situated at over 8,000 feet elevation, which brought near-freezing nights even in the middle of summer. The forests were mostly cedar and aspen, with a few other evergreens scattered throughout. It was a gorgeous spot with three huge, wide-open meadows all coming together at the junction at which was main circle. Nearby, at the edge of the main meadow, was the large fire pit for drum circles.

I spent a lot of time at the drum circles each evening and late into the night. I found that dancing to the pounding, embracing beat of the drums was one of the more powerful healing experiences I came across for channeling the Kundalini energy. The drum circles at a big Rainbow Gathering are truly incredible, and definitely a place to "let it all out" if one feels so inclined.

People collect wood all day long. By evening, when the fire is started, there is enough wood to make a huge bonfire that will last through most of the night. (If fuel starts getting low, then people go on nighttime gathering missions.) Sometime after dinner circle, a few people start the fire, and then the drumming. As the evening progresses, more and more people join the circle until there are dozens of drums—African congas, djimbes, dumbeks, etc.—as well as didgeridoos, flutes, guitars, shakers, tambourines, whatever instrument anyone might think to bring. Hundreds of people gather around the inner circle of drummers, dancing with primal abandon. A space is generally left between the drummers and the blazing fire for those who want to dance close to the light and heat of the flames.

If one were to identify a symbolic representation of the root chakra at the Rainbow Gatherings, then the drum circle would definitely be it—a bright red inferno of flame, pulsing with energy and frenetic activity in the valley of the gathering. No matter where you might be in the nearby forest, from sundown to the early morning hours, you can hear the constant pounding of the drums echoing through the trees.

The pinnacle of the annual Rainbow Gathering always occurs on the 4th of July. It's a distinct alternative to the typical American celebration of Independence Day; but still celebrating the same ideals, namely freedom and liberty, and with plenty of raucous commotion.

Thousands of people gather in the expansive main meadow, around a medicine pole or simple rock design at the center of main circle. Throughout the morning, silence is observed all throughout the gathering site. Many people sit in meditation or else quietly go about their business. A few wander through the converging crowd, burning bundles of sage and smudging (a ritual of clearing a person's aura with sage smoke) those who remain still. It is the one time during the gathering in which the subtle sounds of the forest make themselves known. All that is heard is the rustling of the breeze through the trees, birds singing, feet padding along the dirt paths, and occasional whispers of human speech.

Around noon, the silence is officially broken when a colorful parade of singing children from kiddie village marches into the meadow. People rise from their seated positions to stand holding hands in tight, concentric circles around the center point in the middle of the meadow. At some point a low *Om* sound is begun, and all join in. A profound, deep and constant hum fills the silence, vibrating through the meadow and surrounding forest. Another huge circle of people forms at the farthest edges of the meadow, encompassing the tighter, concentric circles of those surrounding the central pole.

What happens after the group *Om* is always a little different. At this gathering, someone started singing: "All we are saying, is give peace a chance..." And everyone quickly joined in—25,000 people singing in unison, wishing and praying for peace in the world.

Eventually, someone started a drumbeat. From there it progressed into the largest, wildest drum circle and dance jam imaginable. Those in the huge outer circle came down into the center of the meadow to join in the festivities. The drumming and dancing continued all day, through the night, and even into early the next morning before many fell asleep in the grass and dust around the glowing coals of the fire.

I left a week or so after the 4th of July, as the gathering was winding to a close. All considering, I was in very good spirits and was happy to have been able to contribute by being a part of Om Chapati kitchen and to spend time with Jeffrey, Bethany, Forest, Dream, and Marie (who'd arrived there safely a few days after us), and plenty of other kind and beautiful people that I met at the gathering.

I got a ride back west with three rainbow brothers—Marken, Mateo, and Sketch—in a laundry van owned by Marken, that he had turned into the ideal traveling rig. We spent five or six days making our way back towards Oregon, stopping at a few hot springs, and sleeping outside under clear skies in the mountains and deserts along the way.

We arrived in Eugene mid-July, completing a circle from a few months before, when I was just starting my summer adventure. My friend Matt was gone for the summer, so I didn't spend long there. I was excited to be on my way back up to Alaska, after being away for three years. I wasn't entirely sure what I was going to do up there during what remained of the summer. I thought that I might look for a cannery job, or perhaps work in Denali National Park again. But at least I knew one thing—that I wasn't going to have to kill myself to escape what I was going through. The idea had pretty much faded from my memory over the past few months. Though I still had many daily struggles, I was certain that I had the strength necessary to survive this ordeal of spiritual evolution.

I had been accepted to Humboldt State University for that fall, but wasn't sure if I could manage the concentration and dedication necessary for school; and neither was I sure that I was ready to deal with mainstream society while still immersed in the Kundalini process. Instead, I was considering going back to Ananda Village at the end of the summer, to do work exchange there over the winter. It was a spiritually focused and supportive environment where I could wholeheartedly devote myself to my spiritual growth and healing as well as work on improving my back with daily yoga. This was what I really needed. It seemed like the perfect plan for winter.

I left Eugene the same day that we arrived and hitched up Interstate-5 to Seattle. I had a flight already reserved from Seattle to Juneau the following morning and planned to surprise my best friend from college, Erik, who was still living and going to school up there. I'd mentioned to him sometime in the spring that I was thinking of coming up for part of the summer but had never told him that I'd actually reserved a flight. If it turned out that he was gone, then I'd just camp out and then catch the next ferry north. It was just too much fun to surprise people, and it seemed like it generally worked out for the best.

I slept on the hard floor of the airport that night. I got up at 5 a.m. with just enough time to have a hot breakfast and hop on the plane. I got a window seat and sat through the flight musing and contemplating sleepily, watching the forests and sea rush beneath me far below.

CHAPTER 14

As I had hoped, Erik was pleasantly surprised and glad to hear from me when I called that morning to tell him that I was at the Juneau airport. He and his fiancée, Lorrie, were just pondering breakfast. They came down to pick me up and we all went out for breakfast together. Erik and I hadn't seen one another in over a year, so we had plenty of catching up to do.

I spent several days in Juneau with Erik and Lorrie in their apartment before continuing my journey north. Erik came with me on the ferry ride from Juneau up to Haines, Alaska, just south of Canada's Yukon province. We arrived at Haines early in the morning and went out to breakfast together. He then caught the next ferry back down to Juneau, and I continued hitchhiking north towards Canada and interior Alaska.

Though it was great to be back in Alaska amidst the rugged, towering mountains and thick forests of the southeast panhandle, I was beginning to feel, once again, overwhelmed by the whole Kundalini process. I'd felt a certain degree of stability while at the Rainbow Gathering in New Mexico, surrounded by plenty of like-minded souls. But now I was entirely on my own, with things pretty much up in the air, other than a few scattered plans. My uncertain future was now staring me in the face, and that had the effect of amplifying all the usual Kundalini symptoms. This left me having a hard time sleeping, which in turn simply increased my discomfort even more.

Energy, in myriad forms, was backing up within my consciousness, so that I began feeling exhausted, scattered, cloudy, emotionally drained, and in a perpetual state of anxiety. I needed to get all this potent energy moving, but I didn't know how. Good sleep seemed to be an extremely important aspect of the healing process, and yet my sleep patterns were totally out of balance. Some nights I barely slept at all, unable to relax amidst my constant inner conflict. I needed to find a lifestyle that would provide the balance to help me deal with all this on a daily basis, but I wasn't sure what would be the best situation for my rather unique and difficult circumstances.

I still had the option of going back to Ananda at the end of the summer. I held on to this as a potential life raft, anticipating that Ananda would be somewhere I could find genuine balance and centeredness, somewhere I might be able to meet many of my spiritual as well as worldly needs—yoga, good sleep, good food, like-minded company, as well as a routine schedule to help provide some structure to my life. All this swirled through my head as I said goodbye to my friend Erik and continued on my journey into the unknown that lay ahead.

After standing for hours alongside the road at the far end of the small town of Haines, I finally got a ride from a local, about twenty miles north, where I found myself in the middle of the Alaskan wilderness. Aside from the small highway, there were no other signs of civilization. A small creek flowed nearby, and a few eagles flew overhead. The silence, though welcome, was also unsettling in its intensity.

A few hours later, as I was beginning to feel as if I might be the last person left on the planet (a common hitchhiker's paranoia—no one's coming down the road because everybody in the world has mysteriously vanished), I was finally picked up by another local, who took me as far as the Canadian border. I went smoothly through inspections, walked across the border, and then stood just inside Canada for the rest of the day, without getting another ride. As evening descended and daylight waned, I hiked into the nearby woods and set up my tent. I crawled into my sleeping bag feeling lost and depressed, and slept erratically through the night.

The next morning, I got up early and was back on the road. After a few more hours, I was blessed with a ride from a man going all the way to Wasilla, just north of Anchorage, more than five hundred miles away. We drove all through that day and late into the night. He eventually dropped me off at the north end of Wasilla, at three in the morning where, once again, I slept in my tent in the woods just off the highway.

After sleeping in late the next morning and then mulling over my options, I decided to head towards Denali National Park and look for work there. I knew that, as long as there were positions open, I had a good chance of getting hired, since I'd worked there for two summers previously when I was going to school in Fairbanks and Juneau. I hitched from Wasilla north to Denali, arriving late in the afternoon, and then walked with my pack into the personnel office at Denali Park Resorts.

An hour later, I had a job in one of the restaurants, a room in one of the employee cabins with two other roommates, and a little more security in my life. I was lucky to end up rooming with two great guys—Eddie, a musician from Las Vegas, and Chris, a half-Chinese, half-Irish aspiring photographer from Kansas, who had driven all the way up the Alcan Highway alone in his Jeep.

I worked at Denali Park through to the end of their tourist season in late September, two months later. Though I didn't particularly enjoy the work—especially since I got stuck with the early morning shift, starting at 4:15 a.m.—I worked four ten-hour shifts, so at least I had three days off to explore the park.

Chris and I quickly became good friends. We went on a backpacking trip into the park together a few weeks after I arrived. Though it was just for one night, since we had only one overlapping day off, it was great to be back in the heart of the Alaskan wilderness. We took the bus about halfway out to Wonder Lake, a good fifty miles inside the park. I always enjoyed the bus ride. Though it was bumpy, dusty, and seemed to take forever, it was also a welcome decompression chamber on the way out of civilization and into the wilderness.

Once the bus dropped us off, it continued down the road and disappeared over the next ridge, leaving us in complete silence. It was a silence that, I imagine, can be experienced in few places around the world. There were no trees in most of the park, including that area, so the only sound was the gentle dribble of a nearby stream—and the two of us hiking with our backpacks through the thick carpet of tundra down a wide, clear valley.

What is most impressive about Denali National Park is not so much what is there, but rather what is not there. The stillness and emptiness seem at times almost unreal, as if such peace is abnormal, something that can't continue for much longer. Soon, you think, something will have to break the silence. But what that something might be is as intangible as the silence itself, since even the occasional mountain goat, fox, ptarmigan, or grizzly bear off in the distance usually go about their business with little to say. Similar to the desert, the intensity of the Alaskan tundra becomes a mirror, reflecting one's inner self. Just being there can have a tendency to induce a meditative, or at the least contemplative, state of mind.

We filled the quiet with small talk for a little while as we hiked down the valley. Soon we surrendered to the ever-present stillness and continued along down the small stream, lost in our own thoughts, sorting out our lives to some degree (or at least I did). There are no trails in the park, due to the limited amount of people allowed in at a time, as well as the lack of forests. As long as one has a basic sense of direction and a topographic map just in case, it's difficult to get lost. We continued hiking down the valley for a few hours, until it opened into an awesome scene of three huge valleys all coming together.

We set up Chris's tent at a flat spot on the side of a hill and laid out our sleeping bags to nap. Because it was summer, it literally never got dark—just a little dimmer at night—so it was easy to lose track of the time, especially with the overcast skies we were having. We ended up sleeping through the evening and all through the faint light of night. We crawled out of our sleeping bags late the next morning, groggy but fully rested—to find that, almost eerily, nothing much had changed. No glorious sun was there to greet us and welcome the start of a new day. It felt just as it had the previous day when we'd arrived: gray, silent, tranquil, and subtly disturbing.

We ate breakfast, and spent the rest of the morning sitting in the silence for a while; then we did some exploring up one of the wide valleys, just to look around. As morning turned to afternoon, we decided we had better get going, so we could catch the last evening bus out of the park. We took down the tent, packed up, and then hiked slowly back up the valley alongside the babbling stream to the gravel park road. We sat quietly on our packs beside the road until eventually a bus came rolling along to break the silence of nature and deliver us back to civilization.

I felt a sense of completion as I finished my last day of work at the end of September. Although I'd enjoyed tramping around the park, as well as saving up some money, I was looking forward to getting focused on my inner work. I had called the folks at Ananda Village a few weeks earlier and been relieved to hear that they had an opening for me to do work exchange. They were expecting me in mid-October.

Chris was planning to drive most of the way back through Canada down to the "Lower 48" and he invited me to join him, along with another friend from work, Tamara. Since it was the end of the summer season, we were some of the last people to leave the park.

Autumn comes and goes quickly in the far north. The deciduous trees in the lower elevations were now bare. Strong winds blew through the resort as we packed up the Jeep. We sensed that snow would be falling on the ground any day, to stay there until April. The hotel would soon be transformed into another world, very different from that of the bustling tourist season of the past several months. Moose would be strolling through the snow-covered parking lots, and the Northern Lights would be radiating down from above in their multi-colored display.

We left Denali Park and headed north first to Fairbanks, east from there through Tok, across the Canadian border, and then south back down to Haines, where I'd begun my journey a few months before. There we drove onto the huge ferry and, over the next few days, sailed south to Prince Rupert, British Columbia. From there we continued down through southern B.C., to Seattle.

Chris was headed east back to Kansas, and Tamara was going south to Portland. They dropped me off at the Greyhound Station in Seattle, where I caught a bus west out to the coast. I hitched south down Highway 101 through Washington, Oregon, and Northern California and, a few days later, arrived back at my mom's house in Ukiah, feeling almost as if I'd lived a lifetime in the course of one summer.

CHAPTER 15

My brother Christo was taking the fall term off from UC Santa Cruz, to do a bicycling trip around California. He was planning to go to Yosemite National Park first and stay at the same hiker/biker campground where I'd stayed a year earlier. Since I was headed out to Ananda Village near Nevada City (a few hours north of Yosemite) he decided to start his trip from there. My mom gave us both a ride from Ukiah over to Ananda, for us to start our respective adventures. She dropped us off and hugged us tearfully goodbye, wishing us both well on our very different journeys. Christo took off on his loaded bike; and I hauled my few belongings into Ananda's retreat center, my new home for a while.

There were only three others doing work exchange there for the time being, and I was welcome to stay as long as I liked. Since I had no future plans at that point, I assumed that I would stay there through the winter. It was the best atmosphere I could have hoped for, given my unsettling psychological condition. I worked about thirty hours a week—helping out in the kitchen, watering the outdoor plants, sweeping and scrubbing floors, washing the bathrooms, and other odd jobs—in exchange for room and board. I lived in my tent across the meadow from the retreat center for the first few weeks and eventually moved into a small room in a nearby trailer that housed the other workers, as winter progressed and the nights chilled.

There were daily yoga classes at the retreat center, and I also started jogging regularly. Both of these activities proved to be effective in bringing the Kundalini energy more into my body, thus helping me to align with it. I generally shied away from their daily meditations, but found that the simple tasks and chores I did around the retreat center were of great help. Having a routine, a simple rhythm to my life that kept me on task but wasn't overly demanding, seemed to be just what I needed.

I had arrived at Ananda feeling extremely scattered, cloudy, and energetically blocked. The long summer of traveling, although fun, exciting, and adventurous, had also been a whirlwind of activity in which I had for the most part ended up neglecting my spiritual development. And the demands of working forty hours a week in Alaska, especially given the early morning hours, had been draining both physically and mentally, and had also thrown off my sleep patterns. The last few weeks of work I had been dragging myself out of bed every morning, forcing myself through each day, and then lying down to restless nights. But at least I had some money saved up to show for it.

Over time at Ananda, I slowly became a little more clear and balanced, as I was able to attend to and direct my discordant energy patterns. But I still found myself regularly in bizarre, overwhelming mental and emotional states; and was often downright terrified by the intensity of energy flowing through me. I often doubted whether I could handle this experience indefinitely, as it clearly didn't seem that the flow of energy I'd tapped into was going to simply shut off at some point. A year had passed since my initial experience, and yet the Kundalini energy was still commanding my life. It seemed that I was permanently linked to this spiritual reservoir of sorts, and all I could do was get accustomed to it—no matter how I wished at times that I hadn't stumbled upon this challenging and disconcerting phenomenon. But I couldn't look too far down the road. I just had to deal with the present day and take it from there.

Though I was undoubtedly much better now than in the few months following my awakening, the energy's intensity had not, in actuality, diminished at all over the past year. It was as if I had become permanently saddled with a heavy weight. And yet, although that weight was still there on my back, both figuratively and literally, I was to some extent getting used to its presence in my life. The energy was clearly changing over time, and I was changing along with it. Although the power of this force hadn't really altered, my experience of it certainly had. I was beginning to see that this was, indeed, a healing process I was experiencing. Something beautiful was going to come out of this—like an oak tree coming out of an acorn. Much had to be cleared and transformed to make room for the more complex entity—and the acorn had to be patient, as it allowed the mighty oak to grow from within it.

After two-and-a-half months at Ananda, I came to a rather sudden conclusion: it was time for me to move on. Though I greatly appreciated the support and stability of the environment there, I realized, as my symptoms changed and evolved, that the profound intensity of my own process was quite different from that of the gentle daily routine at Ananda. I came to realize that their focus was more on the higher, "upper-chakra" spiritual realms—through prayer, affirmation, visualization, reflection, and meditation. Their yoga was relatively subtle compared to John's intensive class in Eugene, and they seemed to frown on anything that might be considered "primal." It was very different from the path generally recognized at the Rainbow Gatherings, for example, which I found to have more balance between the upper and lower spiritual realms, and more emphasis given to the feeling, intuitive, sensual, passionate, spontaneous aspect of the human spirit.

Kundalini is (as is hopefully fairly evident) a very intense, primal force. And the practices at Ananda weren't getting to the heart of the healing work that I needed. I was simply on a different path. I began to feel that I would be held back in my spiritual evolution rather than aided by staying there much longer. Although the security, good food, good music, kind people and pleasant spiritual routine were hard to leave behind, I simply realized that I needed more room to be myself and more room to follow my own heart and my own unique path.

Following their Christmas celebrations, I packed up my few boxes of belongings and said goodbye to everyone I had met there. They sent me off with the same circle of song that had blessed my departure a year earlier. My mom and step dad happened to be on their way home from Christmas at my aunt's in Reno, so I caught a ride with them back to Ukiah, from which I intended to launch into the next chapter of my journey.

CHAPTER 16

I left Ananda feeling rather confused and overwhelmed. It was now the beginning of a rainy winter. Although I still had some money left from working in Alaska, it wasn't enough to get me all too far down the road, or to put money down on an apartment somewhere. Once again, for better or worse, I had made a leap into the unknown, with little clear idea of where I might land.

After leaving Ananda, I visited my mom for a few days and pondered over my options. I decided to hitchhike up to Eugene to visit Matt and see what might happen along the way. I packed up my worn backpack and was soon back on the road.

Just north of Arcata, I got a ride with a young woman, Janine, who was going all the way to Eugene. She was a high school senior checking out the University of Oregon. She planned to stay in town for a week, before driving back to her hometown of Santa Cruz (where my brother was still going to UC Santa Cruz). Once we arrived in Eugene, she offered me a ride back south in a week, and gave me a local phone number to get in touch with her.

I spent the week in Eugene, staying in a spare bedroom at Matt's house. Though he was glad to see me and put me up for a little while, he was in school and didn't have much free time. I spent most of the week just wandering around town, hanging out in bookstores, reading and writing in my journal in coffee shops, watching people on campus, and going to a few of John's yoga classes. John had become used to my popping into class at random times over the years. I would simply show up, attend a few classes, and then disappear again. I always made a point of attending his class when I passed through town, since I found both his yoga technique and his presence inspiring and uplifting—something I definitely needed while walking my own difficult spiritual path.

I didn't want to wear out my welcome with Matt, so at the end of the week I decided it was time to move on. I called Janine the night before she'd said she was headed back to California and arranged for her to pick me up the next morning. Since she was headed back to the same town where my brother was attending college, I felt that I should pay him a visit. Besides, it seemed like a pretty clear sign for where I should head next. I gave Christo a call to make sure I was welcome to stay with him for a little while. He was glad to hear that I was coming. Janine and I left Eugene early in the morning and drove down Interstate-5 through heavy rain and even some light snow. It happened that my mom and step-dad were out of town right then, and Ukiah was a perfect halfway point, so we crossed over to Highway 101 and made it to my mom's that night. We spent the night there, then continued driving the following day. Janine dropped me off at my brother's place that evening.

My brother lived in a small, wooded trailer park on the UC Santa Cruz campus, in a narrow, short trailer. It had barely enough room for one person to occupy and feel as if they actually had a home, so, it was very generous of Christo to let me stay there with him for two whole weeks. I slept in my sleeping bag on the floor of the trailer, what could be called the kitchen, which allowed barely two feet of space down the center of the trailer. Each morning I'd roll up my camping mattress and sleeping bag so that we had enough room to move around and make breakfast.

As in Eugene, I spent a lot of time just walking around campus, reading, watching movies in the library, and going on hikes in the nearby redwoods. My brother managed to find some time between classes and on the weekend to hang out with me, during which we did some exploring of the local beaches and parks.

After I'd been with Christo for two weeks, I was ready to continue on my way and give my brother back his trailer. The night before leaving, I happened to get a call from Rnu, a co-worker and friend from Ananda Village. She said that there was a Whole Life Exposition going on in nearby San Jose, and if you volunteered then you could get in for free. Barbara Marciniak was going to be doing a workshop there and channeling the Pleiadians. She happened to be one of my spiritual heroes. Rnu was staying with a friend in San Jose, and I was welcome to stay the night as well. The next morning, I said goodbye to my brother, then caught a bus from the UC Santa Cruz campus downtown and hopped another bus over to San Jose.

I had been reading everything I could find on the Pleiadians over the past few months and found myself intrigued by their message and spiritual vibration. The voice and language with which they spoke seemed very rich, deep, colorful, sensuous, warm, and embracing. Unlike many spiritual paths, such as the teachings at Ananda, which tended to preach control of the emotions, desires, sexuality, physicality, passion, intuition, etc., their message was one of embracing and finding balance with these often confusing parts of ourselves. I found that I could relate to this a lot more than the dry, stern, overly intellectual message of many spiritual teachers and teachings. And it simply seemed more human. My quest overall was not to be less human, but rather to be more genuinely human.

I realized, as I sat staring out the bus window on my way to San Jose, that there was something rather synchronous in the fact that I was going to hear the Pleiadians speak. Just a few days before Rnu called, I had woken up in the middle of the night with the distinct impression that metaphysical beings were interacting with me in my sleep. Though the faint impression of this encounter seemed rather dream-like, at the same time I remembered that I had been, in some strange way, more conscious than the typical dream-state—conscious of other, separate entities interacting with me somehow that I could now only vaguely recall. It seemed more than coincidental that I would have this experience on some subconscious level, and then, only days later, go to hear such metaphysical entities speak in the material realm. I found some reassurance in this realization that there was indeed a larger overall plan going on behind the curtains of my individual spiritual process. I seemed to be moving into an experience of life and reality that was becoming ever more interesting, exciting, dynamic, and imbued with meaning, as I progressed with this dynamic spiritual force. It was as if I were breaking down the walls between the conscious and subconscious realms and, in the process, revealing things that were going on "behind the scenes" so to speak, of the visible, outer world. I was beginning to interact with the world on various levels previously hidden to me—or at least, I was becoming more aware of the fact that this was taking place.

I volunteered eight hours of my time at the Whole Life Expo in exchange for free admission, plus a ticket to one workshop of my choice. The Expo reminded me somewhat of an indoor Rainbow Gathering, with a distinctly New Age focus. It was a great opportunity for people watching and, like the gatherings, it drew a wide variety of people, many of them very colorful and out of the ordinary. Although the New Age phenomenon tends to get lumped into one category because of a few commonly shared beliefs, there is really a broad range of doctrines, practices, and values amidst the collection of ideas labeled as "New Age." It includes people from, and thus incorporates aspects of, virtually every recognized world religion, as well as every conceivable belief system *outside* of organized religion.

Many of the people at these events are undoubtedly not very in touch with what consensus calls "reality." Conspiracy theories certainly abound, as well as belief systems that seem founded on little other than personal belief. But many are conversely following spiritual paths that are grounded in ancient practices and are also connected in various ways with the everyday affairs of the world: promoting alternative gardening and energy efficiency, practicing healing techniques such as yoga, massage, meditation, and alternative medicine, affecting global change through politics, law, and humanitarian efforts, and simply broadening the arena of human discourse.

As with all social movements, the so-called New Age phenomenon definitely has its polarization of both positive and negative effects on society. I tended to enjoy these types of gatherings simply because of the abundant diversity of creative energy. I found that I preferred the multi-faceted, oftentimes conflicting belief systems to one rigid, fundamentalist view of the world that I was expected to conform to. The world just seemed too complex to choose one firmly-established, unchanging view of reality, above all the others. Ultimately, it seems that truth, whatever that might be, is easier to discover when there are multiple points of view pointing the way. That's not to say that Jesus, Buddha, Mohammed, Krishna, Zoroaster, and all the other spiritual teachers throughout history don't deserve some respect. But considering that they don't always agree with one another, it seems apparent that there isn't only one way to live a righteous life.

I had never before seen or heard extraterrestrial channeling in person, although I'd read plenty of books on the subject. It completely blew me away. Whether or this phenomenon is real or not, I don't claim to know. But I know that Barbara Marciniak's voice definitely seemed to be speaking from somewhere beyond the walls of the room we were in. I walked out of the workshop feeling almost as if I were an alien myself, a stranger in a strange land. For a short while after her lecture and channeling, I felt like I could hardly talk or make eye contact with anyone. My spiritual vibration was so heightened from the experience that I was afraid that I might freak out anyone I tried to interact with right then.

I ended up wandering around San Jose for a couple of hours, just to get outside and away from the expo center for a little while, staring at the vehicles moving magically along the street, up at the tall skyscrapers, the miles of concrete and bright, flashing lights, feeling as if I'd just been transported to a faraway civilization, in a future time. It was definitely a strange, hi-tech world that modern-day humans had created, when seen from a somewhat shifted perspective. On some level, a part of me wished to be somewhere more genuinely familiar to me—a more natural social environment, in which trees towered over people rather than buildings, and the dirt and grass wasn't contained between narrow strips of concrete. And yet, another part of me was just as fascinated by this fast-paced, technological, seemingly magical world, thankful to be allowed to be a part of it for a time—to learn from it, and hopefully to help in some way affect its future course.

CHAPTER 17

A fter the Whole Life Expo, I made my way via the public transit system from San Jose north back to Ukiah and stayed with my mom and step-dad once again, while I geared up for my next adventure. I was planning a two-week backpacking trip on the Lost Coast—a rugged wilderness area in Northern California, and the longest stretch of coastline in the continental United States without a road alongside it. Although it was virtually in the backyard of my hometown (an hour or so away) I had never been there before. I figured it was about time I checked it out. Besides, it sounded like a good place for some spiritual exploration and contemplation.

After spending a few days doing some work around my mom's place to make a few bucks and then getting prepared for my journey, I packed up and hitchhiked from Ukiah north on Highway 101 to the small town of Garberville at the southern end of Humboldt County. From there, I headed west over to Shelter Cove on the coast.

During my many years of getting around via hitchhiking, I've come to have something of a love-hate relationship with it. There are times—standing in the same spot for most of a day in the pouring rain, while spacious cars whiz by, warm and dry—that make me curse all of humanity, feeling like we're a lost cause if we can't even help each other out when we have the means to do so. When pushed beyond the limits of my patience, I can get so fed up that I seem to enter an altered state of consciousness, in which I lose my desire to hold myself within the normal social limits. As I realize that it's going to be a long while, if ever, until I get a ride, I'll start dancing around alongside the road, making silly faces at passing automobiles, jumping up and down in a wild frenzy, hiding behind my backpack with only my arm and thumb sticking out, singing at the top of my lungs, or laughing uncontrollably—until eventually I wear myself out and resign myself to patiently awaiting a ride.

Other times—too cold, wet and tired to find any humor in the situation—I'll simply close up in a depressed stupor, my arm frozen outwards, thumb extended, praying for a ride to bring me some temporary refuge. In the end, however, I've almost always gotten a ride, at which point I have to admit that I don't blame people for not wanting to pick up a scraggly stranger on the side of the road. Whatever may happen, attempting to hitch a ride from strangers sure can give a unique perspective on society.

But today was a good day to be a hitchhiker. I felt liberated by my freedom to walk out onto the highway, stick out my thumb and catch a ride free of charge, to any destination I might choose (as long as someone else was going there, at least). Though it was mid-February, after months of flooding rains, it was now warm and sunny, and I was exhilarated to be out on the road.

I made it fairly quickly up to Garberville and then west over to the coast. After hopping out of the back of a pickup at Shelter Cove, I hiked a mile up the coast to the beachside trailhead. I set my pack down in the sand, took a seat, and watched the waves for a while as I ate some cheese and crackers, reveling in the sun shining down on me. I removed my boots and strapped them to the outside of my pack to enjoy the feeling of sand between my toes.

I hiked slowly through the sand five miles north along the beach, taking in the sounds of the waves, the clean, salty air, watching the seagulls flying lazily overhead. The sun turned from yellow to orange, and then a fiery red, as it approached the ocean horizon. I stopped at a small creek flowing into the sea and set up my tent on the solid ground just up from the beach. Then I sat down in the warm sand to watch the setting sun and the endlessly crashing waves. Once the sun had gone down, I set up my tent and cooked up some soup on my camp stove. Then I crawled into my sleeping bag for a cozy night's rest.

After sleeping heavily, I awoke to another sunny day. I decided to make the most of the sunshine and spent the day swimming in the ocean and reading on the beach. But conditions changed later that afternoon. A fog bank started to roll in while I was sitting in the sand, reading. I crawled into my tent as the fog poured in. Thick clouds appeared overhead, and it started to mist. By evening it was sprinkling. Eventually, it started to rain.

Though I hoped the storm would pass quickly, I had actually seen the last of the sun for the remainder of my trip. I stayed warm and dry in my tent through that evening. I cooked up some macaroni and cheese on my camp stove and then crawled into my sleeping bag to read my latest metaphysical exploration, *Journey into Oneness*. After a while, I lay down my head to snooze and drifted into pleasant dreams. I awoke the next morning to rain still pelting my tent.

My plan was to spend the first week of my trip hiking north, about halfway up the thirty-five-mile stretch of continuous beach. The second week I would turn around and go southward, along a ridge of the steep mountain range that rises out of the ocean. Since I couldn't carry fourteen days of food in my pack along with all the other necessary gear, I planned to do a three- or four-day fast somewhere along the way. Since it was storming, I decided this would be a good time to stay in my tent and fast. I hoped that it might clear up in the next few days, before I continued hiking.

I stayed relatively dry, if claustrophobic, in my little blue tent, fasting through the next three days as the rain continued to pour down. This was the first time that I had done a fast drinking only water, rather than juice and tea as well. It proved to be a mostly unpleasant experience that I don't intend to repeat—though I did come to some important understandings as a result.

For one, I realized that, since one of my major challenges throughout the Kundalini process was that of staying in my body, fasting didn't have the beneficial effects it had had for me previously. Rather than invigorating and cleansing me as it had in the past, it made me weak and disoriented. This may have been compounded by the lack of nutrients that I would have gotten from juice. Of course the cold, stormy weather and three days of confinement in my tent didn't help much either. I read a lot to distract myself from my growling stomach and slept, though not as soundly as I would have liked. I resolved afterwards to listen more closely to what my body was telling me—what was genuinely helping my emotional and spiritual state of mind, and what obviously wasn't. But at least I did get in plenty of contemplation time, did some journal writing, came up with a few more options for what to do when I was done with this trip, and finished a couple of books. In hindsight, however, I could have still accomplished these things, and with less discomfort, if I'd abandoned my fast when I realized that it wasn't going as smoothly as anticipated.

I was basically worn out by the end of the three-day fast, despite having hardly moved, other than a few brief excursions outside. The rain had continued virtually unabated, so I'd had little motivation to leave the tent. The morning following my first meal I was extremely lethargic—despite having slept ten hours—and found it difficult to fully wake up. Having slept so much already, I decided I'd better get moving—though I wasn't terribly excited about the idea of hiking through the unrelenting rain.

I packed up my things, took down and rolled up my wet tent, pulled on my boots, hefted my pack onto my back, and started hiking up the beach through the storm. It was undoubtedly a different experience than the first day, hiking in the sun barefoot under clear skies. I hiked seven or eight hours along the beach through the pouring-down rain, before I pitched my tent and camped for the night. The next morning, with it still raining, I packed up again and continued along the beach, despite my sore calves and the fact that all my gear was beginning to get fairly damp. Later that evening, as the daylight was waning, I pitched my tent at the base of a small hiking trail that seemed to go straight up the steep coastal mountains. The next day, at the top of that ridge, I would turn south for the rest of my journey, heading back south to my starting point.

In the morning, the rain was coming down harder than ever. It was the eighth day of my trip, and it had been raining for the past six days. I realized that I was in a bit of a predicament. My tent, clothes, and the rest of my gear were becoming increasingly wet since, although my tent was holding up pretty well, I didn't have a waterproof covering for my backpack while hiking. I had no way to dry things out at the end of the day, since making a fire was impossible. Soon enough, my clothing and sleeping bag would be downright drenched, posing the threat of hypothermia.

I checked my somewhat vague Forest Service map and found that the trail leading up the mountain eventually connected with a jeep road, which in turn led to a paved road—though still far from any outposts of civilization. I noted this as a last resort, in case I needed to change the course of my trip. I packed up my damp clothes, damp sleeping bag, and wet tent, and began hiking up the steep grade away from the roar of the ocean.

I hiked up the trail, rising steadily, for what felt like forever. The rain intensified into steady sheets, accompanied by gusts and gales of wind that seemed intent on lifting me right off the trail. I hiked on and on up the steep grade. I stopped mid-day for a brief lunch, then continued along what began to feel like a never-ending trail. Each time I reached the top of a ridge, there was yet another long, uphill climb still awaiting me.

After five or six hours of persistently steep uphill hiking, I finally reached the junction for the trail that headed south along the ridge. This would commit me to another four days of hiking, at least. I was totally exhausted, soaking wet, my pants and boots were drenched, my hands were chilled, and ironically I was now out of drinking water, despite the water falling all around me. The steep angle of the grade had provided no streams along the way, other than shallow rivulets of water flowing through the mud.

I unbuckled my pack and threw it to the ground, then hiked down the trail a little ways to see how things looked. Just as I rounded the first hill, I was greeted by a sudden blast of wind that practically threw me backwards. I took this as a clear enough sign not to attempt another four days of hiking through this ongoing storm. I would risk the jeep trail down to the paved road, in hopes that it would lead me to civilization, and a warm, dry bed for the night.

I checked my map once again and guessed that it was about another ten miles from there down to the paved road. And I was already beyond worn out. But I had little choice other than to hunker down and keep on putting one foot in front of the other. At least I was now at the top of the ridge and it would be mostly downhill from there. I tucked away the map, strapped on my dripping backpack, and continued hiking, despite my sore body, mind, and spirit.

I hiked on and on through the rain. I had no idea of the time of day, with the thick, gray clouds ever-present overhead. After several more hours, it seemed that it would soon be getting dark. I had no idea how much farther I had to go. I decided that I needed to find somewhere to set up my tent before nightfall rather than be caught hiking in the dark. I set my pack down on the gravel jeep-trail—streaked with countless tiny streams, a rather uninviting environment for making camp—to take a look around. But I could find nowhere. The jeep trail was on a steep slope covered with trees, and the trail itself, though wide, was far too wet and rocky to lie down on all night. Besides, I didn't know what condition my tent and sleeping bag would be in at this point. I had to keep going.

I pressed on as the rain continued to fall. At least it was a steady, mild descent, so that it didn't take much concentration or effort to keep placing one foot in front of the other. I went into a trance state of sorts, a hiking meditation in which I lost all measure of time. I no longer felt my tired legs or the water that was dripping down my neck and soaking my shirt. I just hiked and hiked and hiked—hoping to heck that I was actually headed in the right direction. Finally, as the light of day was clearly dimming, I came to the paved road that I had anticipated.

Although this was something of a relief, it wasn't actually much cause for celebration. The problem now—as the map had suggested—

was that the road at this point was still a long ways from anywhere. It was a normal two-lane road, but I couldn't tell where it went to or came from, and there was absolutely no traffic. And my map didn't help at this point, since it was only a map of the Lost Coast.

I made an educated guess and continued hiking along down the road in what seemed to be the best direction, as the sky darkened. After another mile or so, I came to a fork, with a small sign pointing to the right that said "Honeydew." I remembered that Honeydew was also an exit off Highway 101, the main highway running through this area. This was a good sign. So I continued to the right, figuring that I was perhaps thirty miles from Highway 101—and not much farther to Garberville, and a warm hotel room.

It was completely dark by now, and I was starting to get scared. I was completely exhausted physically and mentally, I could barely feel my legs, I was soaking wet, I was cold in spite of the fact that I hadn't stopped moving in hours, and I was pretty certain that everything in my pack was also fully soaked. I kept hiking along, hoping and praying for assistance of some kind.

Finally a car came along. I put my thumb out, but it didn't stop. Not a surprise. Even I would be hesitant to pick up a hitchhiker in the dark, in a driving rainstorm, in the middle of nowhere.

I continued hiking along up the road. Ten minutes later, I saw another car. I waved my arms this time, and they stopped. I explained my situation to the man and his young daughter in the car, and asked if they might be going to Garberville. But they said they were sorry, they were headed home just a few miles down the road, and couldn't help me. I continued trudging along down the darkening road as they drove away, feeling as if my very life force were being sucked out of me as the light of their car faded into the distance.

I was now feeling genuinely desperate. Having no other apparent alternatives, I began looking off the road for somewhere to set up my tent, hoping my gear might miraculously be dry enough that I could survive the night through the storm. As my last thread of hope was fading, and I was about to set off blindly into the dark woods, I saw

a light off in the distance and heard the sound of another car coming. As it came closer, I saw that it was a big pickup truck. I waved
my arms again, as its headlights blinded me through the rain, and it
stopped. Something told me this was the moment I had been waiting
for. I opened the side door of the rusty, beat-up pickup, and sitting in
the driver's seat was a scraggly, older man with a beer in his hand.

"Man, fellah, you looks like you must be wet…" he drawled, clearly a little drunk. He said it purely as an observation—as if he had
pulled over merely to take a look at me, having not yet considered
that I might need help.

"Uh, yes," I said, stuttering through cold lips, trying to speak clearly before he drove off. "You see, I was backpacking at the Lost Coast,
but I quit because of the rain, and I just hiked all day, and I need to
get to Garberville, so that I can find a hotel for the night…"

"Garberville? Shit, that's thirty-five miles! Who you gonna find a
ride with out here at this time of night?" He paused for a minute,
thinking, as if he were trying to drum up a ride for me. "Well heck,
if all you need is a place to stay, you can sure crash at my place…I
mean, it's messy, but at least it's warm, and I got satellite TV and a
comfy couch…"

I had climbed in, my pack on my lap, before he managed to finish
his sentence. At that point I was hardly listening. I sensed that he
meant to help me out, and I accepted without question. That he was
apparently driving drunk wasn't much of a concern at that point. I
was safer in his hands than sleeping through the night in this storm.

We drove another few miles down the road, turned onto a dirt
road, and drove for another mile, finally coming to a fairly run-down,
yet cozy-looking wooden cabin. Though the old man had appeared
a little questionable at first, he turned out to be just a kind, lonely old
alcoholic, who lived alone with his dog in the woods and grew pot
for a living.

The cabin was fairly spacious inside. He suggested that I lay my
things out around the fire so they could dry overnight. I was struck
with both horror and gratitude as I pulled out my sleeping bag, to

find it completely soaked all the way through, literally dripping wet. I realized that I would have been lucky to see morning if I had tried to sleep outside that night.

He cooked up some instant soup, we watched some satellite TV, and then I slept warm, dry and content beside the crackling fire. The next morning, I packed up my dry belongings and he drove me down the road a little ways to a pull-off. I thanked him profusely and then continued hitching towards Highway 101. From there I headed south and arrived finally at my mom's house that evening, grateful for the simple pleasure of a warm shower.

CHAPTER 18

A s usual, I wasn't quite sure what was happening next in my life, though I had a few creative options on the table. I considered flying to Hawaii to work at a communal farm I'd heard of; getting a seasonal job at Big Bend National Park in Texas, or else scraping some money together somehow and moving up to Arcata to get an apartment. Once again, I had applied to Humboldt State University for the fall semester. Moving to Arcata early to get established seemed like a good idea, although school was really more of a last resort at that point. I still didn't feel quite ready to step into that reality.

What I really wanted was to find another spiritual community, along the lines of Ananda Village, where I could get involved with a group of people, plant gardens, make music, find a life-mate to share my adventures, raise children, and be involved in something that felt real and lasting.

Over a few days of pondering the possibilities back at my mom's house, I decided to try and find a place in Arcata, where I would at least be able to get a little more clear and centered as to my future plans. After scraping up some money, in addition to what was left over from the previous summer, I borrowed my mom's car and went up to Arcata for a weekend, got a motel room, and went all over town applying for apartments and studios.

When I got back to Ukiah, I was surprised to find that a letter from Amy was waiting for me. We had been in contact a bit over the past year and had cleared things up since I'd left Austin in a state of confusion. Upon reading the letter, I was blown away to learn that she had just moved to, of all possible places, Arcata. I could hardly believe it.

She wrote that she had gotten sick of Austin and decided to move somewhere else for a little while, just for a change of scene. She had picked Arcata because, when she'd left me in Eugene to go rescue Lisa down in Santa Cruz, she had driven through Arcata, stopped there for lunch, and remembered liking the town. So she had spontaneously packed up her car, driven across the country, found a room in a house with three other guys, and got a job, all in a matter of a couple of weeks.

I gave her a call, and she was equally surprised to hear that I was in the process of moving to Arcata myself. Soon I got acceptance from one of my housing possibilities—a studio apartment building next to the HSU campus. The following weekend I moved into my new home, the first time I had my own place in years.

A few days after settling in, I gave Amy a call and invited her out to the movies. We met downtown and hugged for a long while in front of the local movie theater. I almost didn't recognize her at first, as she had recently cut short her long, dark hair. But she was still beautiful. I was happy to see her again and to have this opportunity to truly resolve things since our troubled time together in Austin. We watched the movie, and then she came over to my studio. We sipped tea and talked for a while, before she biked back to her own place a little ways outside of town.

Over the next few months, we developed a much more open friendship than we'd had previously, even progressing into the realm of romance. Though she worked in Eureka and didn't live right in Arcata, we managed to spend a day or two together each week. I had decided to pay my rent using a credit card, hoping to put off getting a job for a little while. Although my condition was definitely improving, more than a year after my Kundalini awakening I still felt that I couldn't handle working regularly amidst my erratic energy patterns and other ongoing symptoms, so I had lots of spare time to go hiking in the redwoods or to the beach, do yoga, and to hang out in the campus library reading and writing. Keeping my schedule open and fairly simple while I had the chance seemed to be conducive to retaining my sanity.

On a weekend that Amy had free, we decided to go on a little road trip together. She met me at my studio and, with loaded backpacks, we hiked out to Highway 101 at the north end of Arcata, intending to hitch north to southern Oregon and then spend a few nights on a beach together.

We got a ride to Trinidad, only fifteen miles north of Arcata, but then ended up waiting there for a couple of hours without another ride. It became cold and windy as the sun began to go down, and eventually we got tired of waiting. I knew there was a nice beach just a short walk away, even though we hadn't made it far out of town, so we left the highway and hiked down to Trinidad State Beach, surrounded by spectacular rocky cliffs typical of much of the Northern California coast.

Neither of us felt like doing much over the weekend. We lazed around in the sand and sun during the day, did some reading and swam in the cold ocean waves. On the second evening, as the sun was setting, we made a fire to warm ourselves and to cook dinner. After eating and watching the campfire fade into glowing coals, we lay next to one another in our sleeping bags, staring silently up at the stars in the moonless night, feeling soothed by the lulling crash of the waves.

As the night chilled, we huddled together, taking our arms from our sleeping bags to hold one another. We talked quietly, holding each other close, squeezing our bodies together, stroking our hands down each other's backs, and eventually surrendering to the silence, as we kissed. Suddenly it was as if all of the affection we felt for one another, unexpressed over the past few weeks of spending time together, surged forth. Our timidity vanished as we gave in to the passion that had been building beneath our newly rekindled friendship. It was like an electrical charge, yearning to be released, and we allowed it to flow freely between us.

We made slow, sweet, gentle love there under the gaze of the stars and the whispering of dark ocean waves...and then lay quiet and still in the darkness, holding each other close. We slept long and deep through the following morning, curled up together under our pile of sleeping bags. Later that day, reluctantly, we packed up our things and hitched back to Arcata, since she had to work in the evening.

Over the next month or so we continued to spend a few days a week together. Although we shared more physical affection in the form of cuddling and occasional kisses, that was the only time that we made love. We must have sensed that we would part ways soon, and that it was best not to get our lives too entangled. Though we had a strong connection and much love to share, we knew that, ultimately, we had different paths to follow.

I spent part of my time in Arcata researching communes around the western U.S., hoping to visit some during the upcoming summer—perhaps even find one to call home for a while. I'd bought a copy of the hefty Communities Directory, which contained descriptions of over five hundred different communes spread across the country. I eventually found six that seemed like potential prospects, and sent away to them asking for more information. After corresponding over the next few weeks, I decided on two that seemed like the type of community I was looking for.

One was in Sedona, Arizona, called Aquarian Concepts. Their spiritual beliefs centered around a large channeled work known as *The Urantia Book*. I had never heard of it, though I had come across the term Urantia—an ancient name for Earth—in other spiritual texts. I continued correspondence with them over the next month, letting them know that I might stop by for a visit during the summer. They said that I was welcome to come by and visit and participate in some of their group activities, and to call once I arrived in Sedona.

The other community was in Twisp, in north-central Washington, and was called the Methow Valley Collective. It was organized by an older man named Hanson, who sounded like an eccentric, fun-loving character—a paranormal enthusiast, with a good sense of humor. The response I got back from him was a large manila envelope with a friendly letter, a few articles on the community from some local newspapers, some photos of the land, and an assortment of colorful, sparkling plastic stars and confetti that poured out of the envelope as I opened it up. He also said that I was welcome to stop by and visit and to just give a call whenever I rolled into town.

I spent altogether just two months in Arcata having decided not to commit myself to school in the fall. Though it was a brief stay for all the trouble of moving my stuff twice, it yielded some important insights there, and was able to give a little order to my otherwise gypsy life of the past year and a half.

I also was finally able to get into a consistent sleep pattern, in which I had many colorful, complex and intriguing dreams. The sense that I was working with spiritual beings in my sleep became almost a norm during that time. Though part of me felt drawn to contact these beings in a more conscious state—perhaps to learn their identity and my role in relation to them—I was also hesitant to make that leap. As with my experiences in the out-of-body state, I felt that I wasn't yet ready to handle these other realms; and it was better not to get involved in something I didn't understand than to become overwhelmed by it.

Towards the end of May, I started getting the travel bug, curious to check out the two communes I'd selected and see what they were all about. Once again, despite submitting an application, I couldn't quite see that I would be going back to school at HSU that fall. And around that time Amy moved back to Austin to pick up the pieces of her life there, leaving me with little reason to stay in Arcata.

Summer was fast approaching. I also started making plans to attend a music festival I'd heard about in western Washington, at a place called Rainbow Valley. Rainbow Valley was a piece of land outside of Olympia, owned by hippies who lived in buses parked during the winter and followed the Grateful Dead throughout the summer. Since Jerry Garcia had died the previous summer, they wouldn't be following the Dead anymore. Instead, they had a number of festivals of their own scheduled on their land.

From there, I hoped to catch a ride out to the national Rainbow Gathering in Missouri that summer—and visit the two communities I'd researched, either on the way there or the way back. Though I still kept school in mind as a last resort for the fall, I hoped that I would instead be settling down at one of the communities I visited, or else somewhere else that I might discover along the way.

At the end of May, I moved my few boxes of belongings back down to Ukiah, then hitched again up to my studio and spent a few days getting packed and organized and cleaning up the apartment. Then late one morning I turned my key in to the apartment manager and left Arcata for good, hitching north along the coast towards Oregon.

CHAPTER 19

I spent that night in my tent by the ocean just inside the Oregon border and continued north the next morning. At Florence, halfway up Oregon, I got a ride from some students of Evergreen State College—in Olympia, Washington—who were headed back to school after doing a photography project/road trip over the weekend.

Since Olympia was near Rainbow Valley and the students I was riding with said I could sleep in the woods near campus, I rode with them all the way to Evergreen College. Once we arrived, I followed their directions to the nearby forest and soon found a good spot among the trees to set up my tent. I slept there the next two nights and spent the next day checking out the liberal campus. The morning after that, I caught a bus west from Olympia out to Rainbow Valley.

Rainbow Valley turned out to be a fairly ramshackle arrangement, as I had suspected. It consisted of about fifteen old school buses in a dirt parking lot, with a large, open, green meadow down a small hill, across from a creek. There were only a few people there, since the festival didn't start until the following evening. Once I found the owner, he showed me where I could camp and then mentioned that I could help the small crew with setting up if I wanted, in exchange for a free ticket into the show—as I had hoped.

But rather than the mellow, conscious folks I had expected Rainbow Valley to attract, as both performers and audience poured in by the thousands, the quiet, green meadow became what, sadly, felt more like a heavy-metal parking lot party than a peaceful musical gathering. I didn't come across any familiar faces or old friends and was unable to find a ride out to the Rainbow Gathering in Missouri.

Though I enjoyed some of the music, I spent most of the next two days there basically wishing that I were elsewhere.

And then, on the last night of the festival, I was robbed again. I came back from the show to find my tent wide open. The thief had apparently been in a hurry, because my backpack and sleeping bag were still there. They had probably been looking for drugs or money, since other than my rain jacket they had taken only some little bags containing small items. I was relieved that at least I hadn't lost more.

The next morning I woke early, packed up, and got a ride the hell out of there, heading south. I figured I'd head down to Eugene and see what possibilities might present themselves there. I was bummed out that my summer was off to such a rough start and hoped something would come up that would help turn things around. Although I still had most of my essential traveling possessions other than the rain jacket, I simply felt violated by yet another theft. And since I had been unable to find a ride out to the gathering in Missouri, the rest of the summer was looking like a big question mark. Why had this happened, and what did it mean? Was this a sign that I had diverged from my path somehow? Or was it just random karma that I couldn't recognize? Why did these instances of theft happen so often to me? There seemed to be no clear lesson to learn from this incident—just more frustrating pain to endure and, I hoped, quickly move beyond.

The ride that I got out of Rainbow Valley was headed straight to Eugene, about three hours away. I figured I'd probably head from there out to Cougar hot springs and spend a few days soaking and relaxing in the warm waters. After I bought a cheap rain jacket in Eugene, I decided to try and find Jeffrey before leaving town. I knew that he was friends with the owners of Icky's, a teahouse and hangout on the west end of town. After asking around, I was told that he was staying with some folks in one of the apartments right across the street from the teahouse. I walked over and knocked on the door. A red-haired, scraggly-looking guy opened the door and poked out his head.

"What do you want?" he asked.

"I'm looking for Jeffrey," I said. "Is he around?"

"Just a second." He closed the door.

A minute later, the door opened, and there was Jeffrey. I was so happy to see his smiling face. He looked great. Both his hair and beard, like mine, had grown out over the past year, so that he looked more like his familiar, magical, prophetic self.

"Hey, Gabriel!" he said. "What a surprise! What are you up to, man?"

"Oh, same old..." I said as I gave him a big hug. "Just passing through town, you know. Hey, can I take you out for lunch?"

"Well, sure, what the hell...I haven't got any plans. Just let me find my sandals."

After lunch, we walked across town together, since he wanted to stop by a friend's house. I told him about my plans to check out some communities, and about getting robbed.

"Hey, it's just stuff, it comes and goes," he said. "Let it go." Good advice. I did my best. "There's a regional Rainbow Gathering down in Northern California, you know. I'm thinking of going down there for it. It starts in a few days. You should check it out."

I told him I would think about it, and might see him there. After saying goodbye, I caught a city bus about an hour east of town and then hitched the rest of the way up to Cougar hot springs. I spent the next two days soaking in the springs and trying to make up my mind where to journey from there.

I concluded that the gathering Jeffrey had mentioned would be the best place for me to catch a ride out to the big Rainbow Gathering in Missouri. Besides, it would be nice to spend some more time with Jeffrey. The next morning, after another long soak in the springs, I hitched back to Eugene and then, not feeling like getting stuck in town, continued west out to Florence on the coast. I spent the night on the beach again and headed south the next morning, backtracking down Highway 101 to Highway 20, not far from my mom's in Ukiah. But I didn't want to slow down the momentum of my summer quest by stopping by home. From there I continued hitching east, eventually catching a ride to the gathering that evening, in the Mendocino National Forest west of Interstate-5.

The Rainbow Gathering turned out, to my continuing disappointment, to be another uninspiring experience. Despite the surrounding beautiful forest, it was held in a large gravel parking lot accessible to cars, instead of having a hike in to a separate site in the woods. Many of the Rainbow elders had chosen not to attend, because whoever had organized the gathering had apparently obtained a permit for the site, which was against basic Rainbow policy.

The gathering felt more like a bunch of street kids hanging out on the edge of the woods, killing time, rather than a unified group of people focused on healing and conscious togetherness. Without the focus of elders and others more spiritually aware, the gathering lacked intention. They didn't need much help in the small kitchen, and a man with rather heavy, unbalanced energy led the one sweat lodge. And Jeffrey never showed up in the several days that I spent there. His plans, like mine, changed with the weather; he'd probably been distracted by some other happening, or else just wasn't in the mood for an adventure. Though I did make a few friends there, I didn't come across any familiar faces, and didn't feel that I was really contributing to the gathering. I soon began to wonder if I should look for an early ride out to the national gathering in Missouri, or perhaps head straight for Sedona to check out the community there.

I was sitting in the grass one evening after dinner circle, discussing this very question of where to go next with some new-found friends, when I was greeted with some much-needed cosmic synchronicity. I had mentioned my plans to head out to Sedona in passing to another acquaintance. As I was sitting there in the dry grass with a small circle of folks, this fellow came running up to me.

"Hey, Gabriel!" he panted. "Sorry to burst in on you guys, but I just found a ride for you to Sedona, and they're leaving in fifteen minutes! I figured I should at least let you know about it…"

Fifteen minutes wasn't much time to think it over, not to mention take down my tent and pack up. But to have a ride to my potential destination offered just when I was talking about it was a sign I couldn't easily deny—and hopefully a sign that I was headed back in the right direction.

I decided to go for it. I wouldn't be leaving all that much behind. I hugged the folks I'd been talking to, wished them well on their own journeys, and then followed the other friend to the van that was headed for Arizona. He'd just happened to overhear the two drivers talking about leaving soon for Sedona, asked if they had room for someone else, and then immediately came and found me in the meadow. It was an unlikely series of events, but one that my summer, and to some degree my life (or at least that phase of it) would hinge upon.

The ride was with two mellow, friendly guys my age named Natty and Apollo. I had seen them around the gathering, but we hadn't met. After confirming that they were headed towards Sedona that evening and indeed had room in their van, I ran to my tent and packed up my things with lightning speed. It was just getting dark as I hauled myself into the van. We set off into the night.

Natty and Apollo were two musicians from British Columbia, in a large, free-form band known as Down to Earth—a close-knit group of young musicians from the Slocan Valley of southern B.C., Canada, that included an assortment of drummers, didgeridoo-players, dancers, and singers. The band wasn't currently touring, so they were on their own until they met up with everyone else for some gigs later in the summer. Natty was a stocky, dark-haired, dreadlocked didgeridoo-player. Apollo was taller, short-haired and cherub-faced, and a drummer and flutist. They were headed to Sedona for a weekend healing festival to do some didgeridoo sound healings, which was one way they made traveling money when they weren't playing shows.

We drove all night across central California, sharing the driving so we could make it to Sedona by the next evening, in time for the festival the next day. The morning after leaving the Rainbow Gathering, to our frustration, we ran out of gas on Interstate-40 in western Arizona, just past the California/Arizona border. The gas gauge didn't work, and Apollo had apparently lost track of the mileage. After a few hours of waiting in the hot mid-summer sun along the freeway for a tow truck, we were soon enough back on the road. We made it to Flagstaff early that afternoon, and then headed south from there towards the small, spiritual town of Sedona.

About six miles outside of Sedona, coming down a steep grade amidst the red-walled canyons that snake down to the lower elevations of southern Arizona, the motor stuttered to a stop. We had let the van run out of gas again. What a bunch of hippies we were. Since it was downhill, we decided to keep coasting and see how far we could make it. Fortunately, the old van didn't have power brakes. We rolled into the north end of town as evening was descending, thankful to have finally arrived—and not to have to deal with the empty gas tank until the next day.

But the most memorable moment of our overnight, inter-state driving marathon occurred later that evening. We'd decided to stay where the van had come to rest and make do for the night. After hunting down some nearby cheap burritos, we'd all hung out in the van for a little while and relaxed, glad to have nowhere else to go for the time being. A little while later, I was organizing my things before going to sleep in the courtyard of a nearby church, and Apollo was kicking back on the sidewalk, watching traffic, when we heard a sudden exclamation of dismay from Natty, who was going over a flyer for the festival, to find out where in town it was happening the next day.

"Ah, shit, man!" he yelled to Apollo and me from the van. "Shit, shit, shit! This damn thing tomorrow isn't here in Sedona! It's in fucking Sonoma, California! We misread the flyer!"

"No way, Natty—let me see that thing," said Apollo, reaching into the van to grab the flyer. Sure enough, they had confused the names of the two towns, and had driven all night and all day to get to an event that was just a few hours away from the Rainbow Gathering in Northern California.

"Damn!" said Natty, shaking his head. "We're certified idiots! Oh well—what the heck. I always did want to check out Sedona."

They took the news as gracefully as anyone could, especially considering that the whole point was to make some travel money, not spend their money traveling unnecessarily. But of course, it was too late to do anything about it, and they were too exhausted from twenty-four hours on the road to resist reality for long. We all crawled into our respective sleeping bags—I by the church, they in the back of the van—and slept.

CHAPTER 20

S adly, my experience with the commune in Sedona turned out to be yet another painful lesson, in a summer of many lessons. I'd hoped that Aquarian Concepts might be a place where I could finally settle down, commit to something substantial, and focus on inner healing after so much wandering these past few years. They had sounded friendly and thoughtful over the phone, and seemed to have similar ideals and beliefs to my own. In addition, it was an area I'd been curious to check out for a while, having heard about the supposed "energy vortexes" in the nearby canyons, of the beautiful surroundings, and the unique metaphysical vibe of the town.

I gave the community a call the next day. Natty and Apollo needed to deal with refueling the van, so we agreed to meet up a little later to find somewhere to camp. They planned to stay in Sedona for a little while, hoping to still find some clients for their healing work at the local bookstores or other spiritual events.

Though we had only known each other a few days, we felt a mutual brotherhood, a desire to stick together as long as we were on the same path. None of us knew quite where we were going with our lives, and I appreciated their presence, not knowing how things would turn out with the community.

The people at Aquarian Concepts were glad to hear from me. They said they could arrange to see me the next morning. I would meet with a few select members of the community, who would "evaluate" me in some regard, and decide if they wanted to admit me to their Sunday service a few days later. If I passed that test, then I would be allowed to view the grounds of their community. It all sounded a little too formal, but I agreed, saying I would see them the next morning at the address they provided.

After making my phone call and then wandering around town a little in the hot sun, I made my way back to the local health food store to meet up with Natty and Apollo. We bought some food and other provisions and then drove to a free camping area we'd heard about at the north end of town, among the trees and along a river that wound its way down the canyon and then through town.

The following morning we got up early, and Natty and Apollo drove me across town and then out a country road, to drop me off at the house where I was to meet the community members for my evaluation. I knocked on the front door, and a tall, attractive blond woman opened it.

"Hello, I'm Gabriel," I said, feeling a little nervous as I extended my hand.

"Come on in," she said, shaking my hand quickly. "We've been waiting for you."

I stepped inside and was introduced to the three other community members, who sat in chairs forming a semi-circle around another vacant chair, where I was instructed to sit. I set my daypack down on the floor and took a seat, feeling a little wary of the four pairs of eyes staring at me.

They asked me a lot of penetrating questions, and proposed plenty of authoritative answers, on a wide range of topics. They started off with a long discourse on the "true" spiritual history of Earth—before, after, and including the life of Jesus Christ—with an impressive air of conviction. They expressed a number of spiritual beliefs that I was essentially in agreement with: that Jesus was a great spiritual master; that our current era of history was a time of great change and evolution; that ultimately love was the answer to all the world's many problems; and that changing our inner selves was necessary for making any lasting change in the outer world.

I liked some of the things they had to say—what committed spiritual seeker wouldn't agree with many of these beliefs? I'd been reading books expressing similar views for a number of years. And yet, for all their lofty talk, something about them just seemed a little out of whack. This wasn't quite what I'd expected. I wasn't that into rigid formality, and didn't really care much for people who claimed to "know the answers." Although understanding the nature of reality and human history was intriguing and worth investigating, recognizing the underlying mystery of the universe was more important to me than having it all figured out. This group seemed a little too sure of themselves.

I left the meeting feeling perplexed, but with an invitation to come to their weekly Sunday service a couple of days later. I felt torn by my conflicting perceptions and emotions. Either these people were a remarkable group of beings beyond my current spiritual and intellectual grasp, or they were just your standard cult lunatics, who thought they were the center of the universe. I couldn't quite tell. I didn't want to make hasty judgments about people just because they impressed me as being a little freakish. I was something of a freak myself and liked hanging out with unusual characters. I decided to attend their Sunday service, where I suspected I would get a better feel for the community.

I hitched back into town to meet up with Natty and Apollo. We camped at the usual spot that night, in the woods near town. The next day, we drove out of town a few miles to a good swimming hole along the river that had been recommended to us by someone we'd met while hanging out at the health food store. It was a clear, hot day, and the river hit the spot like an ice-cold lemonade. It was fun just to play around in the sun for a day, bullshit, and work on our tans. We camped nearby that night; and the next morning, Natty and Apollo once again drove me into town for my next community meeting.

The commune's Sunday service felt eerily similar to my evaluation, but on a larger, grander scale. More than a hundred members from the community attended, who either lived on their shared land outside of town, or else in the greater Sedona community. They sat patiently in neat rows, expectantly awaiting the arrival of the community leaders: the founder and his wife. The two of them entered through a side door and took their seats on a slightly raised platform at the head of the room, as the entire audience of devotees stood up, bowed and chimed in unison:

"Good morning, prince and princess!"

A select chorus started off the service with an uplifting spiritual song, written by the leader, who gave me a brotherly wink as he recognized me as a newcomer. The rest of the community chimed in and, not knowing the words, I contented myself with looking around the room in fascination at their apparent devotion. There was something about it that was just too orderly, too altogether positive, and too contrived. I found it impressive, as well as somewhat disgusting. They seemed to be keen on proving something to someone, either to themselves, the rest of the world, God, or likely all of the above.

The leader then followed the song with an enthusiastic, lengthy, and self-congratulating spiritual discourse. The followers listened with rapt attention to his preaching against the various evils of society, as well as his affirmation of their own actions and practices as righteous in the eyes of God. Gabriel of Sedona, as the leader was known (not his real name—in fact, no one used their real names), had a colorful and personable style, a charismatic presence that reeked of the message, "I'm a likable guy, who you can be assured knows what he is doing." He came across as a fiercely moral man, but not one constricted to the standard fundamentalist religious ideals that can seem so dry and colorless. His vision was one of a world of great creativity, music, harmony with nature, and abundance, yet all with a humility of spirit, and thankfulness for the blessings of life.

It was a vision that, to some degree, I shared. I too wanted to live in a world of creative expression, beauty and love. Intellectually at least, he had some good ideas. But there was something about his message and his presence—such as the way he had winked at me—that felt too much like a con man selling a miracle cure. As I looked around the room, and later spoke with some of the other members during break, there was something about their energy that just plain creeped me out. They were too much on the same spiritual page, and not illustrating that they were allowed to have minds, and beliefs, of their own.

I left this meeting as confused as before—and with yet another invitation—to come visit their land outside of town a few days later and see the early stages of their community. Even though I was starting to realize it probably wasn't the home I was seeking, I still couldn't say for sure if these people were as crazy as my gut was telling me they were, or if I just had a problem with their level of abounding spiritual positivism. So what if they had high ideals—didn't I? Somehow, I found it hard to accept that an entire group of people could be on a collective course of self-delusion, despite the obvious lessons of history.

That night, back at our river campsite, I made a simple, silent prayer before going to sleep—to God or whoever might be listening—to give me a hand in making sense of this dilemma.

The next morning, the three of us were on our usual route from the camping area into town to go to the health food store for breakfast, visit some bookstores, and see who or what we might run across to liven up the day. Along the way, Natty pulled over to pick up a hitchhiker at the edge of town. As he settled into the seat next to me and we continued down the road, I asked the hitchhiker his name.

"Gabriel," he said.

For a moment I was confused, thinking he was addressing me. Then it clicked: he was just answering my question, as we both had the same name. And then something else clicked, as I realized that it was a trio of Gabriels—him, myself, and the leader of the commune. When I asked a few more questions and discovered that he lived in the area, I decided to ask him if he knew anything about the community.

"You mean those people out on Red Rock Road, Aquarian Concepts?" he said, as his eyes filled with loathing. "Shit, man, that place is a total cult. They're major control freaks, believe me."

He then proceeded to share the story of his mother, who had been involved with the community a few years earlier. She had been a devoted follower, along with her boyfriend at the time, when she unexpectedly became pregnant. But the leaders—who, in some cases, took steps to dissolve couples of which they did not approve—decided that she was no longer fit to be a part of their community.

But for some reason, they wanted her boyfriend to stay. They convinced him to disassociate from her, despite the pregnancy, and continue on as an involved member of the community. She was then banned from attending their services and from the community as a whole, even though she had been a devoted follower and wished to remain so, and was left to deliver and care for the child alone.

This story sent shivers down my spine, and resolved the uncertainty I'd had about trusting my perceptions and gut feelings. This community definitely wasn't the place for me, if there was even a grain of truth to his account. It also left me feeling betrayed, disillusioned, and saddened, that such manipulation could disguise itself as spiritual truth.

I had a brief desire to let the other people in the community know that they were being led down the wrong path. But I quickly decided to let it go and simply end my contact with them. If there was any belief I wholeheartedly held dear, it was that of individual free will. It wasn't for me to decide another's journey. They were free to learn their own lessons. Meanwhile, I was extremely grateful to still have my cherished freedom, to make my own decisions, think my own thoughts, and choose my own destiny.

When we dropped our hitchhiker off in town, I thanked him for sharing the private but well-timed information. Later, after checking out the Aquarian Concepts website and one of their books in a local bookstore, I discovered why I'd had an intuitive reaction against their teachings: their spiritual approach was in many ways the exact opposite of my own. The core of their spiritual practice was the denial of the lower self. This they stated plainly and frequently. Their basic belief was that ascension meant rising above and leaving behind the lower energies and the lower-self emotions, passion, desire, negativity, the body, and even what they termed "self-assertion." Asserting one's self was, in their estimation, a very undesirable quality. And from a cult leader's perspective this makes perfect sense: convince the people that their own views are inferior to that of God and the spiritual elite (in other words, the leaders of the community), and the people will be faithful followers. Instead of encouraging individual discovery, present what has been determined to be the final truth. Everyone present will then have the same basic beliefs, and this will lead to unity, at least if unity means that everyone agrees with one another and, most importantly, agrees with the leader.

This totally flew in the face of my own experience and understanding, as well as that of much of the reading I had been doing: that the spiritual quest and healing process is deeply personal, and that truth is actually relative to the individual. For example, by all accounts I've read, Kundalini awakening follows no standard formula that can be listed and outlined and remedied by one simple program. The process is different for everyone, as each person is different and has differing strengths and weaknesses. So the relevant truth itself differs from one person to the next. In reality, truth is not a constant, defined, stagnant, and concrete conclusion, but rather the meeting point between many different points of view. This is why, in our system of government, a jury of peers must come together in unison to convict a person of a crime. If twelve people from different walks of life can manage to actually agree on something, then there's a pretty good chance that they're onto something, because it doesn't happen that often in the real world. Groups of people will generally find disagreement among themselves, and that's a good thing.

For those people at Aquarian Concepts community who felt aligned with these teachings, perhaps that was the optimum place for them to be and to learn. For them, it was truth, at least in that moment. But for myself, it was all wrong. With a judgment against "self-assertion," I couldn't figure out who I really was in relation to whom I might project myself to be, or others might make me out to be. Their approach seemed disingenuously positive, focused more on a presentation of righteousness and enlightenment, than on the experience of spiritual discovery unique to each individual. My own intention was that of balancing both the positive and negative forces, rather than acknowledging only the positive as acceptable in the eyes of God.

Kundalini awakening in particular is, as I've tried to vividly illustrate, not an altogether positive experience. Much of the process is frightening, painful, frustrating, full of despair and undeniably downcast and negative. Trying to focus purely on the uplifting and positive energies and disconnect from the negative—through meditation, visualization, affirmation, prayer or other means—will serve only to put off connecting with and processing these challenging energies of the so-called "lower self." Of course, these more mental practices can be very helpful, if in practicing them the intention is to find balance. But purely choosing, asking, or commanding oneself to be healed, in my experience at least, does little to actually heal oneself in the long run. The energetic imbalances that we seek to resolve need direct contact that acknowledges them as valid, rather than pushing them aside as negative and undesirable. Ascending into the crown chakra can be little other than an escape from the very real feelings of fear and hopelessness that lie deep in our soul. To bring love and healing to these emotions, and eventually to evolve them, one can't just glance at them and then look the other way; they have to be fully experienced and truly validated.

It didn't take long for me to let go of my expectations of settling down in Sedona; although the traumatic experience did stay with me for a long while afterwards. But after we dropped off Gabriel the hitchhiker, I did my best to simply move on and forget about Aquarian Concepts. It clearly wasn't the place for me.

After breakfast at the health food store, Natty, Apollo and I stopped by some of the local bookstores and came across a flyer for a musical jam session at sundown. We decided to check it out. That evening, we followed the directions a few miles up a dirt road, through one of the small canyons on the edge of town. Soon, we came across some other dusty vehicles parked alongside the road. A few other travelers were gathered nearby, playing drums and guitars around a small fire. We joined them with a drum and a couple of didgeridoos, and played music well into the night. We slept there under the starry night sky rimmed by red rock cliffs.

Someone at the musical gathering told us about some small caves at the north end of town, that sounded like a good place to set up camp for the remainder of our stay in Sedona, however long that might be. We found them the next day after a little adventuring; but they turned out to be more like shallow overhangs in the cliff face than actual caves. But they would make an interesting place to sleep for a while, as a change from our usual spot by the river. The three of us planned to stick around the area a little longer and see what else it might have to offer. We were all waiting for a sign pointing us in another direction.

Natty, Apollo, and I spent that evening talking and watching the stars amidst the mystical desert surroundings; and eventually fell asleep in our separate, dusty little cave-like dwellings, halfway up a cliff on hard red dirt with big, black bugs crawling over us throughout the night.

CHAPTER 21

A week later, I was beginning to feel more as if I were stuck in the Sedona vortex than being transformed by it in any beneficial way. We had been there now for two weeks. But aside from my freaky cult experience, some skinny dipping, sleeping with bugs, and checking out a few bookstores, we hadn't done much of our originally intended canyon exploring, due to an unexplained complacency that was affecting all three of us. And having passed on the commune, I now had even less idea of what was happening in my spontaneous, ungrounded existence than before I'd arrived in this surreal desert town.

I decided that it was time to move on, in hopes that getting back on the road, doing something different, would be a catalyst for inner change as well. Natty and Apollo were staying another week or so, to keep some didgeridoo healing appointments they'd already made. They planned to go to a Mayan ceremonial gathering of some sort at the Four Corners Monument a week later, that they'd read about on another book store bulletin board; and I said I'd think about meeting up with them there. In the meantime, I was going to set my sails and see which way the wind might blow me.

The next day, I packed up and hiked from my bug-ridden cliff dwelling down to the highway at the north end of town, intending to hitch in the general direction of the Grand Canyon. Maybe I would make it down into the canyon this time and have a spiritual revelation that would give me some insight as to where all this was leading.

After an hour of standing with my thumb out, I got a ride to Flagstaff. From there, I got another ride, about fifteen miles further north.

After another hour or so, I started to get tired from erratic sleep, m
merizing traffic, and the warm summer sun shining down on n
at a pull-off on the side of the road. I sat down on my pack wit.
my hitching arm resting on one knee. Feeling pleasantly sleepy, I sat
down on the ground and leaned against my pack with one arm covering my eyes, the other behind my head, and thumb extended, in
case any of the cars whizzing by happened to notice me.

I was just beginning to drift off into an amusing daydream, when a
car pulled over and narrowly missed me. It was three teenagers from
Florida on a summer road trip. I quickly came to from my contemplative daze and climbed into the back of their shiny sedan, pulling
my dirty backpack onto my lap. They were headed for the Grand
Canyon, before making their way back east.

After hanging out for a while on the south rim of the canyon, doing the usual tourist thing, the teenagers invited me to join them for
the night. The four of us camped together that night at a campground
inside the park and cooked up a big pot of macaroni and cheese for
dinner. We roasted marshmallows around the fire and talked triviali-
ties into the late hours. They were a fun group of kids and helped
give me a little momentum to get out of the funk I'd bogged down in
while caught in the Sedona vortex.

The next day—again standing on the rim peering into the depths
of the canyon—I decided to venture on with them. This time, it was
way too hot to hike 10,000 feet down and back up. Maybe next time
the temperature would be just right for my grand trek, but not this
time. The teenagers invited me to join them to Telluride, Colorado,
which they had heard was a nice town to visit. I assured them that
it was, since I had skied there with my family as a kid. I thought it
might be a nice place to revisit a bit of my childhood, as well as camp
in the woods nearby for a few days, before heading to the Mayan
ceremony at the Four Corners to meet up with Natty and Apollo.

We arrived in Telluride at about midnight after twelve hours of driving—to find total madness. It turned out that the next day, unbeknownst

to us, was the first day of the Telluride Bluegrass Festival. Hippies and rednecks were swarming the normally quiet mountain town, as well as festival organizers with flashlights, reflective gear and walkie-talkies directing the masses.

They wanted $30 a night to camp in a noisy, dirty parking lot. This was not only unappealing, but more than any of us could afford. We decided instead to drive into the center of town and see what was happening there. Maybe we would just hang out at a coffee shop and stay awake all night.

But it took almost an hour just to drive the mile into town and find somewhere to park, by which time we were all worn out and fed up with the crowded mess. Rather than try to get back out of town, we parked and decided to look around for somewhere we could possibly sleep for a few hours.

We found a landing at the top of some stairs leading to a local business, where we hoped we wouldn't be bothered until morning. We spread out our sleeping bags and blankets and, exhausted, tried to get some sleep. But, thanks to noise throughout the night and a blinding overhead light that never shut off, we all spent a miserable night on the hard concrete.

By dawn, we were all basically in worse shape than when we'd laid down to sleep five hours earlier. We got up early to avoid being roused by whoever owned the business, and went in search of a good cup of coffee. Hopefully, that would bring us all back to a more manageable state of consciousness. After putting our things back in the car, we wandered down the main street in the early light, until we found a cozy café where we could sit down, relax, and plan out the day—perhaps even find a way to sneak into the festival and have a little fun.

But the coffee following insufficient sleep made me feel like throwing up, and the three teenagers decided, understandably, that things were too hectic in this small mountain town. They were going to continue on their way back east.

I decided that what I needed most was to tend to my psychological and physical health and get some sleep. I was feeling extremely agitated and distressed from the tumultuous events of the past few weeks. My mental, emotional, and spiritual energy was all over the place; it was everything I could do to stay in the present moment. It seemed like I had gotten completely off track from my focused intentions of the spring: to find somewhere to stay put for a while, relax, establish some lasting relationships, and attend to my mental well being. I desperately needed somewhere stable to call home, though I now found myself so far from anything resembling one.

After we'd all finished our coffee, blinked our crusty eyelids enough times, and watched the sun come up to warm the crisp mountain air, we piled back into the car. I rode with them a mile or so beyond the city limits, where I got out and said "thanks" and "goodbye," and they headed off down the road. From there, I hiked up the steep mountain overlooking the town and crowds of bluegrass fans beginning to stir. I set up my tent in a quiet, secluded spot amidst the trees, crawled into my sleeping bag, and slept soundly through most of the day.

Being almost broke, I couldn't afford to buy a ticket and get in to see the show. But there was plenty happening in town, including a small stage where a few bands occasionally played for free. I stayed throughout the weekend festival, sleeping in my tent far from the crowds, then hiking down into town to join in the festivities, have a beer at the local pub, or read in the small metaphysical bookstore.

On Monday morning, as the rest of the festival-goers were leaving, I hiked down the mountain and started hitching back to Arizona. The Mayan ceremony was in a few days, and there was supposed to be a small gathering in the days beforehand, somewhere in the general vicinity of the Four Corners Monument.

The best way to get there from Colorado was to go through New Mexico and the large Navajo Indian reservation that spanned that entire area. I made it to Shiprock that evening, in the heart of the reservation. After a quick dinner at a fast food restaurant, I was back on the road, hoping to get a ride close to the Four Corners before nightfall. Just as the sun was going down, and I was considering hiking out into the desert to sleep for the night, a pickup truck pulled over, with a Native American couple in the front.

"Hey man, hop in the back," said the man in the passenger seat, as he rolled down his window a crack.

I threw my pack into the back of the truck, and saw that they already had a couple of riders, a young man and woman also with backpacks, leaning against the back of the truck cockpit.

"Hey, you guys, how's it going?" I said as I climbed in, recognizing them as fellow wandering souls. I was elated to have some company for the ride—and even more so when I found that they were headed to the same Mayan ceremony a few days later. It turned out that the Native couple driving the truck belonged to the family who owned the land around Four Corners, and they both worked there. They invited the three of us to sleep on their land out in the desert that night, and said they could give us a ride straight to the monument the next morning.

I leaned against my pack in the back of the truck as we continued down the road, thankful for more synchronicity as guidance and protection—and yet feeling simultaneously overwhelmed. Things in my life were happening too fast, making me feel like they were completely out of my control. I felt carried along by some invisible force, and I wasn't altogether sure that it was taking me where I wanted to be. I needed to just stop my constant movement and rest, without worrying about where I was going or what I was doing next. I wanted to simply *be*—in the present moment—for a long while. But I didn't know how to find or create a place where that was possible. I wasn't even sure if that which I sought was possible to be found, period. I wasn't sure where I was going, I wasn't sure how I would get there, and I didn't know if I would recognize the right place when I got there anyway.

After driving miles through the desert beneath a beautiful starry night, we eventually arrived at the couple's home, a trailer parked in the middle of the vast desert. They made dinner for the three of us weary travelers, and then led us outside to sleep in their "guest room" next to the house—a simple adobe structure with a leaf-covered roof.

In spite of the peaceful desert surroundings and the soothing sounds of the leaves overhead, I awoke feeling extremely cloudy and disoriented. I felt as if my whole world were caving in on me. I was lost in the heart of unfamiliar country. I was almost broke, waking up on a stranger's land a thousand miles from friends and family, with no idea where I was going or what I was doing with my life. Despite the dry desert earth beneath my feet, I felt as if I had no ground on which to stand. What was the point of all these seemingly endless travels? Why couldn't I just find somewhere to call home? Must it be so hard to find peace and happiness? On some level, I knew precisely what it was that I was seeking, but I didn't know where it was, when I would find it, what exactly it would look like, or how much I would have to go through to find it. Maybe that which I was searching for was right around the next corner. Maybe it was in the next lifetime. Everything just seemed totally up in the air.

After breakfast with the kind Native couple that morning, the three of us rode in the back of their truck about an hour to the Four Corners Monument. Soon, we tracked down the small camp of folks a mile from the monument, where people were gathering for the upcoming ceremony. I came across Natty and Apollo, as I was looking for a good camping spot and, glad to see them, set up my tent near their van for the night. Although I'd only known them a few weeks, they seemed at that point like old friends. We spent the evening catching up on our past week of travels and discussing the Mayan ceremony the next morning.

Though I tried my best to get into the spirit of preparing for the upcoming event—an auspicious day representing the dissolution of borders between humanity, as designated by the esteemed Mayan calendar—my consciousness was definitely elsewhere. Once this was over the following day, I needed to decide where I was going next. I still planned to make my way up to Washington to visit the other community, but I felt little certainty that it would work out, given my experience in Sedona and everything else that seemed to be off-course in my unsettling life predicament.

The half-day ceremony attracted more than three thousand people—impressive, considering the remote location. But because neither my mind nor heart were truly present, its significance passed me by. Instead I was looking expectantly down the road, praying for guidance and protection through whatever might be next on the horizon.

That afternoon, following the brief ceremony, I hugged Natty and Apollo goodbye, saying that I hoped we might meet again someday, though I had no idea when or where that might be, since none of us had addresses or phone numbers to exchange. As it turned out, they were actually planning now to go to the Rainbow Gathering in Missouri. But for some reason I felt that wasn't the right direction for me. I got my backpack out of their van, where I'd left it through the ceremony, and was soon, once again, on the road.

CHAPTER 22

I hitched north into Colorado and made my way back to Telluride. I spent another three days there, sleeping again in the woods just outside of town, savoring the peace and quiet of nature now that the festival was no longer going on. The first night, arriving late and feeling intolerably road-weary, I crawled into my tent, collapsed inside my sleeping bag, and slept deeply for more than twelve hours. It felt as if I were unconscious for days.

I awoke feeling unusually refreshed and revitalized, experiencing a powerful stream of invigorating energy flowing throughout me. A much-needed night of deep sleep had worked wonders for both my physical and spiritual being. I just lay there through the morning, taking it all in, feeling the cells of my body being nourished by this powerful energy flowing *through* my soul, for a change, rather than ramming into it. My basic daily difficulty wasn't that I didn't have energy—it was that I was too often carrying around energy that wasn't in motion. Rather than putting this force to use, I was instead being dragged down by it, because I had such a hard time aligning with it.

The distinction between feeling this energy moving rather than its being a dead weight was truly a world of difference. Though it was still intense, as usual, it was an entirely different experience when I managed to actually find balance with this source of energy. I felt more in command of it, rather than the other way around. It actually felt good for a change, in that moment, to be channeling the profound Kundalini fire. On those occasions when I was able to find the eye of calm amidst the storm of my life, I was reminded why it was worth facing all the pain of connecting with this dynamic energy:

because it offers a deep and reassuring presence when allowed to flow freely through one's being. It is the life force energy, and feeling it makes one feel more alive and more at peace. It is a peace based not on leaving one's lower self behind, but instead on finding balance and resolution with it—as they say, oneness between the yin and the yang, recognized as equal and essential aspects of one unified circle of consciousness. Union between these two forces, rather than separation, brings about a deep and real satisfaction of being fully present, fully whole, fully here and now.

The union of the rainbow—of high and low energies, positive and negative, masculine and feminine, centered in the heart, grounded in the root, enlightened in the crown—is the eventual purpose and ultimate goal of the awakening Kundalini energy. Kundalini is the biological force that has the power to bring human consciousness out of its fragmented and diminished state and into brilliant and vibrant wakefulness. This force exists like a sleeping, coiled serpent in every human soul. Whether or not we allow it to awaken within us and honor and align with its purpose, is up to us. We can choose denial and unconsciousness, or we can choose to experience the glorious potential of our fully conscious awareness. I don't claim to actually be at that point yet; but of course, my hope is that at least I'm traveling down the path in the right general direction.

After another night of deep sleep in the woods near Telluride, I continued hitching north through Colorado, spending the chilly nights alongside the two-lane highways. There were a number of places along the way where I thought I might be stuck hitchhiking for days, since I was taking small roads with little traffic, traversing the remote parts of Colorado as I headed for northern Washington. But always, some kind person would come along after a few hours, just as I was beginning to wonder if my guiding light had abandoned me.

I turned west into Utah, where I splurged on a campground one night, and decided to shave my now-bushy beard, just for a change. Afterwards, I looked five years younger. But it was good to see my face again. Besides, it would undoubtedly help my chances hitch-hiking.

I continued north into Wyoming, passed through Jackson Hole, and arrived finally at Grand Tetons National Park. I had last been there on a cross-country trip with my aunt when I was eight years old, and I'd always wanted to visit there again. I thought I might look for some seasonal work there, since I could use some more traveling money; or at least do some real backpacking, since I had all of the necessary gear along with me.

I was dropped off inside the park by a man who pointed me towards a campground that he'd thought, for some reason, was free. This seemed unlikely inside a National Park, but I figured it was worth investigating. Sure enough, when I hiked up to the attendant, I found that it was $10 a night, as I had expected. Having only about $150 to my name at this point, this was a little beyond my budget, since I planned to stay in the area for at least a few days.

Across the road from the campground was a huge, sage-filled meadow, with a small forest of aspen trees perhaps a quarter-mile from the road. I climbed over the barbed-wire fence and walked out to the grove of trees. It was perfect. It felt like an oasis of trees in a wide-open valley—shady, with a soft, clean grassy floor amidst the sparse trees. It seemed the ideal place to rest for a while. I figured that if I were careful, I would go unnoticed and have no lasting impact on the area.

I set up my tent so that it was hidden from view, then pulled out a pouch of tobacco, which I smoked very occasionally when on the road, and rolled up a cigarette. I sat against a log in the grass, blowing smoke rings into the air, relaxing in the silence, allowing my mind to wander, now that I'd found somewhere pleasant to rest for a little while. I spent the next four days mostly just hanging out in the little grove, contemplating, sleeping, reading, writing, and sorting out both my thoughts, and my plans for the future.

After my respite, I left a small bag of unnecessary items tucked under a bush in the grove, got a camping permit from the nearby ranger office, and then spent another five days in the back country, hiking high up into the Grand Tetons. Though usually it didn't bother me, I found myself a little concerned about encountering bears—perhaps because I was informed of one nearby on my first night, right in the middle of cooking up a big pot of chili. But by the last day of back-packing, the fear had mostly left me as I became more open and at-tuned to the calming, comforting vibrations of nature.

I came out of the woods feeling clear, centered, and focused. I decided not to look for a job in the park after all; it wasn't what I re-ally wanted to do with the rest of the summer. I felt strongly that my next step was to go investigate the community I'd previously corre-sponded with in northern Washington. I was being urged in that di-rection. I had a sense that another valuable lesson awaited me there, and that it would be more rewarding than my previous experiences of the summer.

I continued north through Yellowstone National Park and into Montana. Once I reached Interstate-90 I made it rapidly west, leav-ing Montana and crossing the thin finger of northern Idaho. About halfway through the state of Washington, I left the Interstate and went north.

I slept that night at an abandoned spa resort beside Soap Lake in Central Washington—a shallow, pristine lake imbued with naturally occurring minerals, which apparently gave it healing properties that had made it a sacred place for the Native American tribes of the re-gion. I slept in the grass at the lake's edge, took a cold, invigorating swim the next morning, then continued hitching. I figured I would make it to Twisp (the closest town to the Methow Valley Collective) by that evening, sleep near town somewhere, and then give the folks at the community a call the following day to see if I could come by for a visit.

That afternoon, I got a ride from a kind, middle-aged woman and her daughter, who took me to Chelan Falls, about an hour from Twisp. The woman invited me over to her house for a late lunch. Of course I agreed, always grateful for kindness from strangers while traveling. At her house she served me up a large helping of hot, homemade lasagna.

As I was about to say goodbye and continue hitchhiking, she remembered that a friend of hers was actually headed to Twisp in about an hour, and was stopping by her house first. I could probably just hop a ride with him, if I didn't mind waiting. Though I felt a little impatient to get to my destination, something told me to take the ride; besides, it would probably be quicker than taking my chances hitching.

She had a few cherry trees in the back, and told me I could pick as many cherries as I wanted while I waited. She gave me a paper bag, and I went around to the orchard behind her house to fill it with sweet, juicy cherries. Eventually her friend showed up, who was going to Twisp to run an errand. He was more than happy to give me a ride.

On the way to Twisp, munching the cherries as we cruised along through the gorgeous Washington forests, I mentioned that I was going to sleep in my tent near town that night. He said he knew of a great camping spot just outside of town where he could drop me off. I said that would be great, since I hadn't known where I was going to camp.

We arrived just as it was getting dark. He dropped me off about a half-mile before town, at a small dirt road that led into some trees and down to the Twisp River. He pointed towards the best place to camp back in the woods, and I thanked him and waved goodbye, as he drove off towards town.

As I was walking down the narrow dirt road, I had to go around a station wagon and a pickup truck that were parked in the middle of the road. A small group of people was busy loading a large rubber raft onto the back of the truck, having apparently just finished up rafting down the river.

As I passed by, I nodded and said hello to one of the men, who was tying down one side of the raft. He nodded and smiled back at me and then spoke up.

"Hey, you aren't about to camp back in those woods, are you?" he said.

"Well, yeah..." I said tentatively. "Someone told me this was a good spot. Why, is camping here illegal or something?"

"Oh, no, it's a designated camping area alright. But it's about the worst place you could choose to camp out right now. The mosquitoes are horrible this time of year. As you can see, they're already getting pretty bad, and once that sun goes down, they'll practically eat you alive...But hey, if you need a place to sleep, you could stay up at our place, if you like."

"Uh, where's that?" I asked, intrigued, but wary. "At your house, you mean?"

"Well, you see, we've got a little farming community forming up in the hills around here, and we're looking for new folks to come and help us out on the land. You could stay for a night or two in one of our little wooden domes, and then check out the community while you're up there, I mean, if you're interested. It's a beautiful area just a few miles out of town, good company, good food, good music, no head-trips or anything, we're pretty down-home folks really, just work hard and play hard..."

I was speechless for a moment. I was tired out, feeling a little depressed, glad that the long day of traveling was over—prepared for little else than sleep. I was expecting to just set up my tent in the woods, crawl into my sleeping bag, and fall gratefully into unconsciousness. But now this...

"Well, yes, I am interested. That's actually why I'm passing through town. I'm up here to check out a commune. What's yours called, anyway?"

"Okanogan Farm."

"Oh," I said, a little disappointed. It would have been awfully convenient if it'd turned out they were part of the same community of folks I'd come there looking for. "Well, there must be two communities around here then. But sure, I think I will take you up on your offer, what the hell..." At least I wouldn't have to deal with setting up my tent, not to mention the mosquitoes. Besides, here was yet another community for me to look into, and these folks seemed pretty nice.

"So, what's the name of this other community around here, then?" the man asked, as he finished tying on the raft.

"Uhhh...the Methow Valley Collective," I said.

He looked at another guy standing next to him, and they both laughed.

"Why, is it some weird cult, or something?" I asked, confused by their response.

"No, it's not a cult—that's us! We're also known as the Methow Valley Collective. This is the Methow Valley we're in—Okanogan is the name of our organic farm, where most of the people live, but not everyone. You must have talked to Hanson. He actually lives in town."

I was dumbfounded. "You know Hanson? You guys are part of the Methow Valley Collective? I can't believe this!"

"What's your name, fellah?"

"I'm Gabriel. Man, this is amazing!" I stuck out my hand. "What a crazy coincidence, that you guys would be right here where I was dropped off, when you were who I was looking for."

"Yeah, no kidding...I'm Rob. It's nice to meet you," he said, shaking my hand with a firm grip. "And this is Richard."

"Nice to meet you," said Richard. "Go ahead and climb in the back with the raft, and we'll give you a lift up to the farm."

"Great—thanks a lot, you guys!" I said, feeling both overjoyed and overwhelmed.

"Hey, no problem," said Rob, smiling as he climbed into the cab of the truck.

I sat in the back of their pickup as we drove slowly into the small mountain town of Twisp, then turned west and continued up a long, winding road that curved up into the hills.

I could hardly believe what was taking place. The timing was so perfect—it was as if they had been waiting there for me to show up. Of all the mysterious synchronicities that had occurred over the summer and past few years, this one was really blowing me away. In that moment, I knew with certainty that I was guided, that I was protected, that I could trust the universe to bring me whatever I might need or want in life, simply by allowing it to work its miracles through me.

On some level, I was creating my own reality here, I was responsible for this—and for everything else, both beautiful and painful, that had occurred in my life these past few whirlwind years. How could I not believe that there was something strange and miraculous happening in my life, and in the world? I was experiencing it at almost every turn, no doubt about that. And yet somehow, I felt certain, I was also making it happen.

This was the art of being, what I was experiencing right here and now. I only had to look around to see that something of profound significance was taking place both around and within me. The planet was transforming in some subtle, deep, mysterious way. And I was changing along with it. My soul was evolving into something I could hardly comprehend—though I could see it beginning to emerge from within me, like the bud of an acorn reaching for the sky.

What would I be like when the change was complete, if it ever was? How long would it take to find true peace and balance? What would I feel like when that happened? What would I do with myself? Would life be truly different then, compared to now? How would I know for sure when I had arrived, so to speak, at the right place, at the right time?

Though the questions plagued me, I knew that, for the time at least, finding the answers didn't really matter. Right now I was in this moment, in this human body. The most important thing was for me to simply *be* there. As long as I was rooted in the soil of the moment, the sun would continue to shine, the rain would fall, and nutrients would be provided as I needed them. As long as I was willing to learn from life's myriad lessons, then I would be guided—one way or another—and would grow, over time, into the fullness of being.

AFTERWORD

I've wandered through a lot of new territory from where this story ends, both within and without. I lived on the farming community in the Washington Cascades for the rest of that summer; which undoubtedly provided many valuable learning and growing experiences. Then, ready to move on, I continued my travels around the West that fall, with a friend that I'd met while on the farm; went to Hawaii for the winter and lived for several weeks in the rainforests of the Kalalau Valley; spent most of the following summer living at another commune in Montana; lived in my tent for a month in the redwoods of Northern California; and then headed back to Hawaii again for the winter, where I lived for half a year on yet another farming community.

In the fall of 1999, I journeyed to India—the metaphorical origin of Kundalini and of spiritual illumination—and delved to the depths of that profoundly rich and vibrant culture. Upon my return five months later, I decided to resume my college education, and finally received my B.A. in World Religions two years later, from HSU at the heart of the redwoods in Humboldt County, California.

The adventure within has been equally as exciting and challenging. The force of energy flowing through me has never really abated. It has simply changed and evolved in subtle ways. And I've done my best to transform along with it, so that my experience of its presence has gradually shifted. Although in one sense, I am basically the same person as before all of this occurred, at the same time I'll never be quite the same. Kundalini seems at various times to be both a blessing and a curse, depending on my perspective from one day to the next. It often feels like a weight; and yet, any weight is simply

171

energy in some form, which can be tapped into and utilized, once understood and directed.

Kundalini, as I understand it, is the primal universal energy of life and of consciousness. When properly aligned within one's human spiritual and physical being, it has the power to change your mind, like nothing else can. It is the fuel for the soul, the fire of sustenance that provides for us throughout our lives, and beyond. We all need some measure of this life-giving spiritual energy in order to survive, whatever you might choose to call it—Kundalini, chi, prana, spirit, etc. The measure in which we allow it to move through us and invigorate our body, mind, and soul determines to some extent how alive we really are.

With all that said, I wish to emphasize a word of caution to spiritual seekers interested in experiencing for themselves this flow of vital energy. Please do not try to force the awakening of Kundalini, as the results (as is hopefully apparent by my story) can be dangerous. If possible, find a teacher with experience in the matter who can help guide the process. Or else, simply remain open to the possibility of such a spiritual awakening occurring naturally and allow it to happen of its own accord, at the right time.

They say that the universe never gives you more than you can handle. I'm not entirely certain that this is true; but looking back, it seems that I was able to handle what I was given, so hopefully this is indeed the case. It's always a risk when facing the darkness of the unknown. But someone must be the first to venture beyond the known boundaries. And I believe it's worth the risk to find out what's out there, or in there, as the case may be. Just remember to take a look before you leap. And safe travels.